"[A] short and elegant history of the early growth of libraries."—Amy Schwartz, *Wilson Quarterly*

"This wonderful book assembles much of what is known about libraries from caches of Sumerian clay tablets to the foundation of monastic libraries in the 7th century A.D. . . . Not just a fascinating tale of the contributions of Aristotle, the Alexandrian Library of Ptolemy, the great private and public libraries of Rome, this slender book considers from a most apt vantage point the nature of education and culture."—*Virginia Quarterly Review*

"Diverting and instructive."—Michael Dirda, *Washington Post Book World*

"Casson's book is not limited to where and when important libraries existed, it offers a social history transcending the idea of a library as we know it. . . . As appealing to the archeologist as the bibliophile."
—*Publishers Weekly*

"Utilizing his tremendous scholarship in history, archaeology, and the classics, Casson paints a fascinating picture of literature, literacy, and the development of libraries through Greek, Roman, and early Christian times. . . . Casson's book is a wonderful trip into a literary world that bears a striking resemblance to our own."—John Steingraeber, *Ruminator Review*

Libraries in the Ancient World

Libraries

in the

Ancient World

LIONEL CASSON

YALE NOTA BENE

Yale University Press/New Haven and London

First published as a Yale Nota Bene book in 2002.
Hardcover edition first published by Yale University Press in 2001.

Copyright © 2001 by Yale University.

For information about this and other Yale University Press publications, please contact:

| U.S. office | sales.press@yale.edu |
| Europe office | sales@yaleup.co.uk |

Printed in the United States of America

The Library of Congress has cataloged the hardcover edition as follows:

Casson, Lionel, 1914–
Libraries in the ancient world / Lionel Casson.
p.   cm.
Includes bibliographical references and index.
ISBN 0-300-08809-4 (alk. paper)
1. Libraries—History—To 400.   I. Title.
Z722. C37   2001
027'.09—dc21   00-011668

ISBN 0-300-09721-2 (pbk.)

A catalogue record for this book is available from the British Library.

10 9 8 7 6 5 4 3

To Judy

Contents

Preface

This book is the first full-scale study of libraries in the ancient world. It presents whatever is known about them from their debut in the ancient Near East in the third millennium B.C. down to the early Byzantine period, the fourth and fifth centuries A.D., when the spread of Christianity and of monasticism fundamentally changed the course of library history.

Ancient writings contain only haphazard bits of information about libraries. To fill out the picture we must turn to a variety of sources. One of the most helpful is archaeology: at a number of sites excavation has laid bare library remains, and these give us an idea, in some cases a fairly good idea, of the physical facilities. Inscriptions relating in one way or another to libraries, from decrees honoring wealthy benefactors to epitaphs on the gravestones of humble employees, provide welcome detail on important aspects. But there are certain matters, such as the nature of the holdings in the various libraries, the readership they served, the way they made their acquisitions, their methods for shelving and cataloguing, and so on, for which we are reduced to inference based on faint clues, or even, at times, to pure speculation.

The book is addressed to both general readers and scholars. For the latter I have supplied, in a section at the back, complete documentation; it is keyed to the statements concerned by means of page references and brief clues rather than footnote numbers to avoid the distraction these can cause.

It was Harry Haskell of Yale University Press who suggested the idea of a book on ancient libraries, and I am deeply grateful for his stalwart support during all the time it took to bring it to fruition. My good friend N. Lewis, author of the fundamental study of the manufacture of papyrus paper, was kind enough to check my statements on that subject.

The book is dedicated to my wife whose encouragement, as always, was unfailing and who, as always, passed a keen and critical eye over the manuscript.

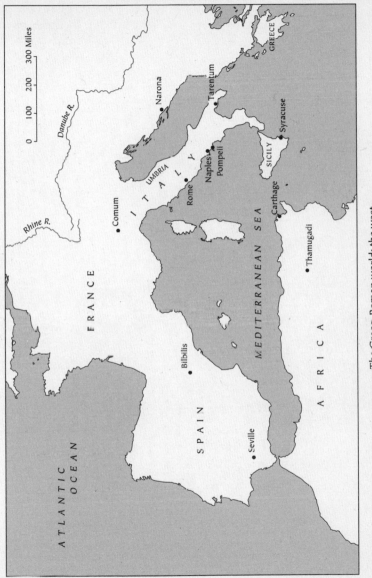

300 Miles

200

100

0

Danube R.

Rhine R.

ATLANTIC
OCEAN

FRANCE

SPAIN

• Comum

• Bilbilis

• Seville

GREECE

Narona •

Tarentum

UMBRIA

Rome •

Naples

Pompeii

MEDITERRANEAN SEA

I T A L Y

SICILY

Syracuse •

Carthage •

AFRICA

• Thamugadi

The Greco-Roman world: the west.

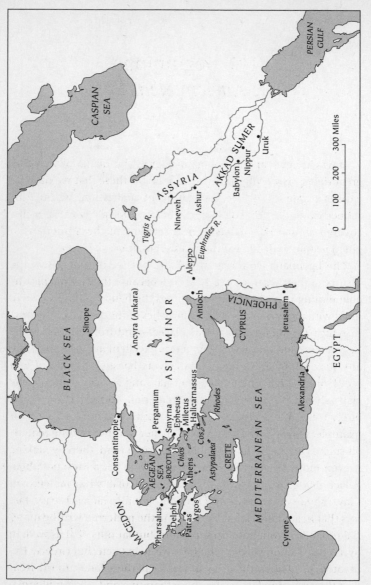

The Greco-Roman world: the east.

1

The Beginnings
The Ancient Near East

It was in Egypt and Mesopotamia, lands abundantly watered by great rivers, that civilization arose. And it is there that we find the earliest examples of that key feature of civilization, writing: inscribed clay tablets that date shortly before 3000 B.C. have been discovered among the archaeological remains of the Sumerians, a gifted people settled in southern Mesopotamia.

The Egyptians were not far behind, but we cannot follow the history of their writings nearly as well because they used a perishable writing material. In ancient times the banks of the Nile were lined with papyrus plants—the bulrushes of the "ark of bulrushes" in which the infant Moses was placed—and from the reeds the Egyptians made a form of paper; it was excellent in quality but, like any paper, fragile. Mesopotamia's rivers boasted no such useful reeds, but its land did provide good clay, and as a consequence the clay tablet became the standard material. Though clumsy and bulky it has a virtue dear to archaeologists: it is durable. Fire, for example, which is death to papyrus paper or other writing materials such as leather and wood, simply bakes it hard, thereby making it even more durable. So when a conqueror set a Mesopotamian palace ablaze, he helped ensure the survival of any clay tablets in it. Clay, moreover, is cheap, and fashioning it into tablets is easy, factors that helped the clay tablet become the preferred writing material not only throughout Mesopotamia but far outside it as well, in Syria, Asia Minor, Persia, even for a while in Crete and Greece. Excavators have unearthed clay tablets in all these lands. In the Near East they remained in use for more than two and a half millennia, and in certain areas they lasted down to the beginning of the Christian Era until finally yielding, once and for all, to more convenient alternatives.

The Sumerians perfected a style of writing suited to such a material. It consists basically of simple shapes, just wedges and lines, which could easily be incised in soft clay with a reed or wooden stylus; scholars have dubbed it cuneiform from the wedges (*cunei* in Latin) that are its hallmark. Although the ingredients are merely wedges and lines, the combinations of these to form signs standing for sounds or words number in the hundreds. Learning them required long training and much practice; inevitably, literacy was by and large limited to a small professional class, the scribes.

The Akkadians conquered the Sumerians around the middle of the third millennium B.C., and they took over the various cuneiform signs used for writing Sumerian and gave them sound and word values that fit their own language. The Babylonians and Assyrians did the same, and so did peoples in Syria and Asia Minor. For the scribes of these non-Sumerian users of cuneiform, training was doubly demanding. The literature of the Sumerians was treasured throughout the Near East, and long after Sumerian ceased to be spoken, the Babylonians and Assyrians and others kept it alive, the way Europeans kept Latin alive after the fall of Rome. Their scribes, as a consequence, had to know the values of the various cuneiform signs for Sumerian as well as for their own language.

The contents of the earliest clay tablets are simple notations of numbers of commodities—animals, jars, baskets, etc. Writing, it would appear, started as a primitive form of bookkeeping. Its use soon widened to document the multitudinous things and acts that are involved in daily life, from simple inventories of commodities to complicated governmental red tape.

Archaeologists frequently find clay tablets in batches, sometimes batches big enough to number in the thousands. The batches consist for the most part of documents of the types just mentioned: bills, deliveries, receipts, inventories, loans, marriage contracts, divorce settlements, court judgments, and so on. These records of factual matters were kept in storage to be available for reference—they were, in effect, files, or, to use the term preferred by specialists in the ancient Near East, archives. Now and then these files include pieces of writing that are of a distinctly different order, writings that do not merely record some matter of fact but involve mental activity. They range from simple textbook material to creative literature—and they make an appearance very early. Near Nippur in southern Mesopotamia, for example, excavation brought to light a group of tablets, dating to the middle of the third millennium B.C., on which were inscribed lists of geographical names, lists of gods, lists of professions, writing exercises, a number of hymns. They could well be from a collection belonging to a school for scribes, perhaps one maintained by a temple, a collection of works that were kept handy for consultation—in other words, its library.

Around 1980 archaeologists working at the site of ancient Ebla in Syria, thirty or so miles southwest of Aleppo, while digging out the remains of Ebla's royal palace, had a stroke of phenomenal good luck: they came upon its main archive room filled with some two thousand clay tablets that were on file there when, around 2300 or 2250 B.C., invaders set the palace on fire. The room was a rectangle roughly 3.5 × 4 m, and the tablets were found in heaps on the floor. Apparently they were kept on wooden shelves along the walls and, when the shelves burned through, the tablets fell down. The great majority were administrative records: almost a thousand pieces listed distributions of textiles and metals by the palace authorities, while another hundred or so had to do with cereals, olive oil, agricultural land, breeding of animals. But, along with these was a group of tablets whose contents were totally different. There were some sixty on which lists of words in Sumerian were inscribed—names of professions, of geographical locations, of birds, of fish. There were twenty-eight with bilingual lists, in Sumerian accompanied by translation into Eblaite. There were more than a dozen incantations, some in Sumerian and some in Eblaite. And there were two tablets—duplicates—with the text of a Sumerian myth. The excavators have determined that they must have come from a top shelf along one wall, the north wall of the room. The clear implication is that, shelved amid the palace records, was the working library of the palace scribes.

Ebla's collection was small enough for users to consult by simply browsing through the shelf of tablets. As collections grew larger, this would at some point cease to be feasible. Modern libraries meet the problem by drawing up catalogues of their holdings—and so did the scribes of the ancient Near East. Among the tablets found at Nippur were two, dating to around 2000 B.C., both inscribed with a list of Sumerian works of literature—various myths, hymns, laments. One, slightly longer, has sixty-eight titles, the other sixty-two. They clearly have to do with one and the same collection because forty-three titles appear on both. The longer has twenty-five titles that are not on the shorter, which, in turn, has nineteen that the longer lacks. It could well be that the two lists arose because the scribes catalogued the collection involved—perhaps a batch of tablets in a given area—at two different times, the second time after a re-shuffling that removed a sizable number of works and replaced them with others.

A catalogue, even so primitive a type as the one embodied in the Nippur tablets, a mere listing of titles in no consistent order, was a notable step toward systematizing a collection. Two further steps were improved cataloguing and the adding of identifying notes to tablets. Both of these steps had been taken by at least the thirteenth century B.C., as can be seen in finds from Hattusas.

Hattusas is an ancient site, located two hundred miles or so southeast of Ankara, which was the capital of the empire of the Hittites from the seventeenth to the thirteenth century B.C. Here archaeologists uncovered a huge mass of tablets that came from the royal palace there. Inevitably most are of documentary type connected with governmental activity, but there are a good number that are not, ranging from prosaic handbooks to Hittite renderings of Sumerian and Babylonian epics. Some of these have, added after the end of the text on the back surface, several lines of writing that identify the work more or less the way a title page does today, the colophon, as it is called; the term is derived from the Greek word *kolophon*, "finishing touch," reflecting the ancient practice of providing as a "finishing touch" at the end what we provide through a title page at the beginning. Here are a few examples:

> Eighth tablet of the Dupaduparsa Festival, words of Silalluhi and Kuwatalla, the temple-priestess. Written by the hand of Lu, son of Nugissar, in the presence of Anuwanza, the overseer.

> Third tablet of Kuwatalla, the temple-priestess. Not the end. "When I treat a man according to the great ritual" [i.e., the first line used as title].

> Second tablet of Tudhaliyas, the great king, on the oath. End. This tablet was damaged; in the presence of Mahhuzi and Halwalu, I, Duda, restored it.

Each colophon begins with the number of the tablet it is on. This was of vital importance, for, though the scribes wrote on both faces of a tablet, and often wrote very small, many works required more than one, even as works today require more than one page. But tablets, unlike pages, could not be bound; the best that could be done was to keep them together, either in stacks on top of each other or on edge alongside each other, both of which arrangements left ample opportunity for individual tablets to get misplaced or lost. The colophon often includes, as in the first example, the name of the local scribe who copied the text. The third example involves a tablet that had come from elsewhere and had suffered damage; it records the scribe who took care of making it usable.

Not all tablets had colophons. Where they were present, they unquestionably were of great help to users of a collection: a glance at a colophon immediately revealed a tablet's contents and the part of the work it represented.

A discovery at Hattusas reveals that catalogues had come into existence that were a great advance over the bare listings in those found at Nippur. The discovery was of a series of tablets, probably belonging to the thirteeth century B.C., that contained detailed bibliographical entries. Each entry begins by giving the number of tablets that made up the work being recorded, just as modern catalogues give the number of volumes in a multi-volume publication. Then the entry identifies the work itself by giving the title, which may take the form of citing its first line, or by giving a capsule description of the contents. Then it tells whether the tablet marked the end of the work or not. At times the entry includes the name of the author or authors, or adds other useful information. Here are some samples that illustrate the nature of the entries and their variety:

> Three tablets on the spring festival of the city of Hurma. How the presiding official celebrates the festival. First and second tablets missing.

> Single chapter. When the singer in the temple of the deity Inar breaks the offering bread he then recites as follows in Hattic. The end.

> One tablet. Words of Annana, the old woman. When one supplicates the Storm-God. Not the end.

> Single chapter. Words of Ammihatna, Tulpija, and Mati, priests. . . . When in a cultic place in a temple that is pure one finds fraud, here is the ritual therefor. The end.

> One tablet on the fine oil of Azzari, the Hurrian woman doctor. When one leads the troops in battle against an enemy city and a charm using fine oil is put on the general who commands the army, one anoints the general, his horse together with his chariot, and all his battle gear. The end.

> One tablet, the end, on the purification of a murder. When the exorcist-priest treats a city for a murder. Words of Erija.

> Two tablets. When the king, queen, and princes give substitute-figures to the Sun-Goddess of the Earth. The end. However we have not found the first tablet belonging to it.

> Words of Ehal-Tessub. . . . When for a man his male and female slaves do not get along, or a man and a woman do not get along, or a man and a woman see bad dreams; how one carries out to Istar (?) the magic ceremony of the evil hatred.

In addition to noting missing tablets, the entries now and then provide information about shelving. There is an entry, for example, which in listing a work that happens to be in two tablets notes that "they do not stand upright"; presumably, in the part of the palace holdings represented by this catalogue, most tablets were stored on edge while these two, exceptionally, lay flat.

A good number of the works recorded in the entries have turned up in the unearthed mass of tablets. Some of these have colophons that are similar in wording to the entries—indeed, one colophon corresponds, word for word. Quite possibly the compilers of the catalogue, as they passed along the shelves, saved time by simply copying or paraphrasing colophons whenever they came across them.

Practically all of the works listed in the catalogue have to do with religion: ceremonies for public occasions, rituals for a variety of circumstances from putting a protective charm on a general headed for combat to solving a domestic quarrel, interpretation of omens, and so on. Indeed, the subject matter is so consistently of this nature that the sudden appearance, right in the middle of a series of entries about rituals, of one listing a work on a treaty between the king of the Hittites and some local ruler may well reflect an ancient instance of mis-shelving! The holdings of the palace at Hattusas were, to be sure, far from being limited to such materials; they included myths, legends, historical annals. The catalogue, it would seem, was of one particular collection that, to judge from the contents, was for use by the palace clergy. It would have been an invaluable tool: any priest who needed a ritual for a given problem, instead of picking up tablet after tablet to read the colophon if there was one, or some lines of text if there was not, had only to run an eye over the entries in the catalogue. It was a limited tool: the order of the entries is more or less haphazard (alphabetization, for example, lay over a millennium and a half in the future) and they give no indication of location. But it was, no question about it, a significant step beyond the simple listing of titles of the Nippur tablets.

The finds at Hattusas, in short, reveal the development of procedures for organizing a collection of writings. The palace holdings were certainly extensive enough to require them: the catalogue alone, representing, as we have seen, just the clergy's working library, lists well over one hundred titles. Now, modest collections of tablets were to be found throughout the Near East, for they were a natural result of the way scribes were trained. The key element was repeated copying of well-known works, so every master had on hand a collection of these to serve as models, and his students could build up collections of their own by simply keeping some of the copies they ceaselessly turned out. Scribes associated with temples by the same assiduous copying built up collections for their temples; the scholarly material served the scribes themselves and the religious, the temple priests. It was in this fashion and not by purchase that collections were put together, for a book trade does not seem to have existed in the Near East.

On the other hand, a library the size of that at Hattusas was strictly a prerogative of kings, all-powerful figures who could create holdings en masse by plundering the collections in places they conquered or, when that recourse was not available, by sending out the palace scribes to copy whatever was desired. Which particular monarch was responsible for Hattusas' library or for any of the previous royal libraries, such as Ebla's, we do not know. It is not until the end of the twelfth century B.C. that we can finally cite the name of a founder of a library—Tiglath-Pileser I, one of Assyria's greatest rulers, whose reign lasted almost forty years, from 1115 to 1077 B.C.

The proof was unearthed in the ruins of the temple of Assur, Assyria's chief god, at Ashur, the nation's religious capital. Excavators found in a certain area there numerous tablets that seemed to belong together: the writing is similar, the nature of the clay is similar, and a number of sure indications of date point to their having been assembled during the reign of Tiglath-Pileser I. It has been convincingly argued that they were part of a library that he created, possibly while he was still crown prince. Some one hundred different works can be ascribed with a fair degree of certainty to it, a number that surely represents only a part of what the holdings were in his day. As at Ebla and Hattusas, only a handful of these are purely literary; most are the professional writings that were the indispensable tools of scribes and priests. The biggest component were works dealing with omens, the determination from stars and other heavenly bodies, from sacrificial animals, natural events, and the like, of what lay in the future. The next biggest were standard handbooks—vocabulary lists, list of plants, trees, animals, gods, place names, a multiplication table, an astronomical text. There were some hymns—and even a catalogue of musical compositions, whose entries went so far as to include the instruments they were to be sung to, for example:

> 5 Sumerian psalms comprising one liturgy, for the *adapa* [probably a tambourine].

> Song to the reed flute in Sumerian.

> Three recitations to the pipe in Semitic.

Thus, if scholarly inference is right, to Tiglath-Pileser I goes the credit for being the first founder of a library whom we know by name. It is, however, a later king of Assyria, Ashurbanipal, who, no question about it, was founder of a library. Moreover, what he founded "has every right to be called the first systematically collected library in the ancient Near East." In size it was many times greater than any before and was not to be surpassed for the next three and a half centuries.

Ashurbanipal, Assyria's last important ruler and one of its most noted, held the throne for well-nigh half a century, from 668 to 627 B.C. He was himself literate: he boasted not only that he achieved "the highest level in the scribal art" but that "among the kings, my forerunners, none had learned such an art." During the latter half of the nineteenth century, British archaeologists working at Nineveh, the royal seat of Ashurbanipal and his predecessors, came upon a vast quantity of tablets in the ruins of two of his palaces. The find turned out to be a treasure trove: it has provided, over and above hundreds of examples of the various types of professional writings, the texts of the Epic of Gilgamesh, the Epic of Creation, and most of the other noted works of ancient Near Eastern literature that we possess today. Colophons provide the link to Ashurbanipal. Some read baldly: "Palace of Ashurbanipal, King of the World, king of Assyria." Others are long and detailed:

> Palace of Ashurbanipal, King of the World, King of Assyria, who trusts in Ashur and Ninlil, whom Nabu and Tashmetu gave wide-open ears and who was given profound insight. . . . The wisdom of Nabu, the signs of writing, as many as have been devised, I wrote on tablets, I arranged [the tablets] in series, I collated [them], and for my royal contemplation and recital I placed them in my palace.

1.1 Clay cuneiform tablet, 14.6 cm × 13.3 cm, with the Assyrian version of the Gilgamesh epic. From the palace of Ashurbanipal at Nineveh.

The library was founded for the "royal contemplation." It was, in other words, the king's private collection, one he could exploit personally since he had mastered what normally was limited to professional scribes, the ability to handle the "signs of writing," that is, to read and write cuneiform.

In the mass of tablets unearthed at Nineveh there were, as usual, archival documents mingled with library material. The library material shows more or less the same mix as in Tiglath-Pileser's holdings. By far the largest component were omen texts. The next largest was the technical literature of religion and magic—rituals, incantations, prayers, and the like, for warding off evil or calling for divine aid. The next largest were scholarly texts—lists of cuneiform signs with their readings, lists of words and names, dictionaries for translating from Sumerian into Akkadian. The tablets bearing literary works such as the Epic of Gilgamesh, so prized today, were but a handful in comparison. It has been estimated that Ashurbanipal's library contained about 1,500 titles; since many existed in multiple copies, in some cases up to six, the total number of tablets was much greater.

How did Ashurbanipal gather his collection? In 648 B.C. the successful completion of a war against his half-brother who was ruler of Babylon gave him free rein over affairs in that great cultural capital. He helped himself to tablets in the temples there, loaded them into carts, brought them to Nineveh, put them in with his other holdings, and, on top of that, had copies made of them. He took tablets from Tiglath-Pileser's library in Ashur. And he took tablets from private collections. We learn this from an unusual discovery, fragments of the record of a large accession made, as can be deduced from certain chronological clues, between January and March 647 B.C. The entries, though many are lost or incomplete, supply invaluable information. A number of them, for example, state the source of the acquisitions, as in the following instances:

2 [i.e., tablets] lamentations.
1 [i.e., tablet] The Dream Book.
In all, 125 tablets [i.e., including

122 listed in previous, lost, lines].
Arrabu, an exorcist from Nippur.

1 one-column tablet,
Anti-witchcraft.
Musezib-Nabu, son of Nabu-sum-iskun,
scribe of the King of Babylon.

The tablets listed in these entries must have come from the personal collections of the men named; similar entries show other such collections being tapped. Ashurbanipal's agents probably confiscated the tablets involved or put in a royal "request" for them. It looks as if owners turned over writings that were not directly connected with their profession and hence more easily dispensed with. Arrabu, for example, an exorcist, gave up a work on the interpretation of dreams rather than, say, something on driving out demons, and Musezib-Nabu, son of a scribe and presumably one himself, gave up a work on witchcraft rather than a vocabulary list or the like.

The new accessions, estimated at around 2,000 tablets and 300 wooden boards, represented a significant acquisition (and the inclusion of boards is a reminder that Near Eastern collections contained works on this form of writing material as well as clay tablets, and that whatever was on them has been lost). The date, early 647 B.C., was right after Ashurbanipal's victory in the war that gave him control of Babylon; this sizable addition could well have been part of the plunder.

Although the library was for Ashurbanipal's use, certain others—his personal secretaries, for example—must have had access. This led to trouble, judging from the following colophon:

Clay tablet of Ashurbanipal, King of the World, King of Assyria,
who trusts in Ashur and Ninlil. Your lordship is without equal,
Ashur, King of the Gods! Whoever removes [the tablet], writes
his name in place of my name, may Ashur and Ninlil, angered
and grim, cast him down, erase his name, his seed, in the land.

Several other colophons have almost identical threats. Ashurbanipal's library, it would seem, was troubled by what so many of today's libraries are—theft of holdings. The king's answer, in accord with the spirit of his times, was to call down the wrath of god on the culprits. He also did what is more in accord with the spirit of modern times: he introduced security measures. A text in the collection indicates that consulting a "tablet of the king" took place from beginning to end before a royal official ("whoever opens the document shall close it in his presence").

Ashurbanipal's library, housed in the royal palaces and available to a limited few, had to deal only with theft. Less restricted collections suffered the gamut of library ills. The evidence is provided by the colophons of a number of tablets—omen texts, lexicographical matter, rituals, and the like—that were found in Ashur and Uruk and date roughly from the reign of Ashurbanipal's father down to the third century B.C. They very likely come from collections belonging to schools, which perforce allowed access to students, or to individuals who may have granted it to fellow professionals.

Some collections offered the privilege of borrowing, and this brought in its wake the inevitable problem of ensuring prompt return. An omen tablet from Uruk insists that "He who fears Anu, Enlil, and Ea will return it to the owner's house the same day." Another is less strict: "He who fears Anu and Antu will return it to the owner's house the next day." One way to avoid the problem was not to let any holdings leave the premises. Thus a ritual tablet from Uruk warns that "He who fears Marduk and Sarpanitum will not entrust it to [others'] hands. He who entrusts it to [others'] hands, may all the gods who are found in Babylon curse him!"

Then there was the danger of maltreatment by users. Some tablets bear a simple caution: "He who fears Anu and Antu will take care of it [the tablet] and respect it" or "[The tablet] by order of Anu and Antu is to remain in good condition." Maltreatment could go so far as to render the text unreadable—the ancient equivalent of the modern desecration of tearing out pages. And so there are injunctions stating "In the name of Nabu and Marduk, do not rub out the text!" or "Who rubs out the text, Marduk will look upon him with anger." A tablet from Ashur with a list of maxims has a colophon that identifies a variety of ways of maltreating a tablet and invokes the wrath of every god in the heavens on offenders: "He who breaks this tablet or puts it in water or rubs it until you cannot recognize it [and] cannot make it be understood, may Ashur, Sin, Shamash, Adad and Ishtar, Bel, Nergal, Ishtar of Nineveh, Ishtar of Arbela, Ishtar of Bit Kidmurri, the gods of heaven and earth and the gods of Assyria, may all these curse him with a curse which cannot be relieved, terrible and merciless, as long as he lives, may they let his name, his seed, be carried off from the land, may they put his flesh in a dog's mouth!"

And then there was theft, the problem that affected even Ashurbanipal's library. A number of tablets from Uruk carry the warning "He who fears Anu and Antu will not carry it off by theft" or "He who fears Nabu will not carry it off by fraud." Others offer a twist on this: "He who carries it off, may Adad and Shala carry him off!" Tablets found at Ashur call down a variety of punishments on "he who carries off this tablet": "May Shamash carry him off," "May Shamash carry off his eyes," "May Nabu and Nisaba . . . render him deaf," "May Nabu decree his destruction." One is more detailed: "He who steals it by theft or takes it by force or has it robbed by his slave, may Nabu . . . spread his life like water." Even temples were robbed, to judge from the colophon of a lexicographical tablet that the owner had deposited in the Eanna temple at Uruk as a votive to Ishtar to ensure his health and long life: "The scholar who does not steal the document and replaces it in its holder, may Ishtar regard him with joy. He who makes it leave the Eanna, may Ishtar denounce him with anger."

The offenders against whom these threats were directed were scribes and priests and other such professionals. Their needs were the reason for being of all Near Eastern collections, whether the royal collection at Ebla or Hattusas or the private collection of a Uruk scribe. Ashurbanipal's library, for all its size, was no different: it was, to quote a noted Assyriologist, "a reference library geared to the needs of the diviners and those specialized practitioners of magic who were responsible for the spiritual security of kings and other important persons. To this were added several sets of handbooks for educational and research purposes, meant to maintain the scholarly standards and the technical proficiency of these essential professions." It has even been suggested that the library was geared to one specific need of one specific person, the king himself. In Ashurbanipal's day, imperial policy was very much directed by omens, and the king had about him counselors who recommended given actions based on their interpretation of these, backing up what they offered with citations from the appropriate literature. Since colophons state that the tablets were for Ashurbanipal's "royal contemplation and recital," "for study in his reviewing," "for study in his reading," could it not be, the suggestion runs, that the library existed in order to enable him to carry out personally the crucial matter of checking the accuracy and aptness of the citations.

Whatever its exact purpose, Ashurbanipal's collection, like all others, was, a professional reference library. What, then, were the purely literary works doing there? There was only a handful of them, and they could well have been there for the same reason as the rest of the holdings, for use by professionals. The Epic of Creation, for example, was read during the celebration of the New Year; the Epic of Irra was held to be helpful against plague; the myth of Atrahasis, a Noah-like figure, was thought to help in childbirth.

In sum, Near Eastern collections were of a specific nature that answered to the needs of the civilization of which they were part. They ceased to exist when that civilization came to an end; they were not the seed which engendered the libraries with their far wider horizons that were to arise in the world of Greece and Rome. Nevertheless they deserve honorable mention in the historical record. They were the first to use some of the fundamental library procedures: the identification of individual works through titling; the gathering of similar works into series; the creation of catalogues. And they were the first to suffer from some of the fundamental library ills: theft and abuse of the holdings.

A final word about the other center of civilization in the Near East, Egypt. Though it produced a rich body of writings, both technical and literary, it has nothing to add to the history of libraries. They existed there, to be sure, but we know of them only vaguely and indirectly. The one bit of specific information we have comes not from Egypt itself but from an account of the land written long after its great age had passed by a Greek historian of the first century B.C., Diodorus. In describing the building complex of "Ozymandias"—his name for Ramses II (1279–1213 B.C.)—Diodorus tells that it included a "sacred library" and even cites the inscription this bore, "Clinic for the Soul." It sounds as if it was a library of theological writings—but we will never know, for the Egyptians, as we noted at the outset, wrote on perishable papyrus paper, not clay, and, although numerous individual specimens have survived, the large masses that might represent a library's holdings have not.

2

The Beginnings
Greece

The libraries of the Near East, of limited scope and purpose, were a far cry from the library as we know it, with shelves full of books on all subjects and doors open to readers with interests in all subjects. Such a library had to await the coming of the Greeks. For they were a people endowed with what was needed to bring it into existence—a high level of literacy and an abiding interest in intellectual endeavor.

As it happens, when the Greeks first appear in history, during the Mycenaean Age as historians call it, roughly 1600 to 1200 B.C., they were more like their contemporaries in the Near East. This is the age reflected in the epics of Homer, in whose narrative the land is ruled by all-powerful monarchs holding court in impressive palaces amid the trappings of great wealth, the likes of Agamemnon and Menelaus. For long the picture he presented was thought to be the stuff of mythology. Then, in the nineteenth century, archaeologists began to unearth remains that revealed the sober reality behind Homer's words—the ruins of massive city walls, of many-roomed palaces, of mighty tombs. They even found writings. The language was an early form of Greek but, as in the Near East, the writing was on clay tablets and in a syllabic form of script. Thousands have been excavated from the palace ruins. To the great disappointment of the discoverers, none were literary in content; without exception they were humdrum records presumably connected with palace administration.

Around 1200 B.C. a series of events brought an end to this period of Greek history with its royal splendors. The cities were destroyed or abandoned, and the knowledge of writing was lost; its purpose had been to serve the palace administrations and, when these ceased to exist, it did too.

A dark interval followed. Then, in the ninth century B.C., the curtain rose on the age that was to produce drama, history, philosophy, and the other celebrated Greek intellectual achievements. In the course of time it produced a by-product of these accomplishments—the library that was progenitor of today's.

But first a series of essential preliminary steps had to be gone through. To begin with, the Greeks had to relearn how to write. Sometime before the beginning of the first millennium B.C., the Phoenicians developed an alphabetic form of writing. Around the middle of the eighth century B.C. the Greeks, who at this time had well-established trade contacts with the Phoenicians, borrowed it and adapted it for their own language. As we have noted, the various forms of cuneiform, with their multitudinous signs, required long and arduous training, and writing consequently was limited to a professional class. The alphabetic script that the Greeks devised, with two dozen or so signs capable of rendering every word in the language, made the path to literacy quick and easy.

That was the initial step. Others equally important had to follow. Schools had to be established to spread the knowledge of reading and writing. Enough people had to go beyond that basic skill to build up a literate class of meaningful size. Enough of its members had to indulge in reading for other than utilitarian reasons to foster the writing of books. And the demand for books had to grow enough to give rise to a book trade. Once books were commercially available, the literary-minded were able to build up collections— and the private collection was the precursor of the public library.

There is endless wrangling over exactly when these steps took place and, more important, how much of the population each affected. The problem is lack of hard information. There are only straws in the wind to go on, and most of these happen to concern not all of Greece but the city of Athens alone. Fortunately, during literacy's formative years Athens was the cultural center of the land.

For the fundamental question of just how widespread literacy was among the Athenians, an answer has been sought in the dramas of Aeschylus, Sophocles, and Euripides, which from the middle of the fifth century B.C. to its end held pride of place in the city's cultural life and were viewed by audiences that included the entire citizen body. Those who believe there was widespread literacy claim that the audience must have been literate, for otherwise certain scenes would have been incomprehensible. They cite Euripides' play *Theseus,* in which at one point an illiterate herdsman describes a complex of lines drawn on a sail that he sees in the distance and, as he does, the audience becomes aware that the lines being described form letters that spell out the hero's name. Those who believe there was only limited literacy reply that such a scene proves merely that the audience's competence went far enough to spell names but that very few were capable of much more. They insist that word of mouth, the sole means of communication before the introduction of writing, by no means gave way immediately to the written word but for long continued to play a key role. They give as prime examples the *Iliad* and the *Odyssey.* Composed to be recited, they were so presented by specially trained bards and continued to be recited by such bards long after the alphabet had come to Greece. Indeed, the poems were probably not set down in writing until a full two centuries after that, about 550 B.C., and then only to stabilize the text, not to serve readers.

Be that as it may, by 500 B.C. Homer's verses were most likely being read, and not only his but those of other poets as well. Greek vases provide the proof. There are a number, some of which date as early as 490 B.C., that are decorated with scenes showing a person seated on a chair holding an open roll and reading from it. Occasionally the artist includes letters or words on the roll, at times so meticulously that they can be made out. In one picture the words are from one of the Homeric hymns; in another, an imaginary portrait of Sappho, they are from one of her poems.

Were there many such readers? That involves another related question: Were there schools for teaching the skill? If so, did they

2.1 Greek red-figured cup, 490–485 B.C., with a picture of a teacher
holding a roll. The writing is a line from a poem by Stesichorus (active
600–550 B.C.). The artist, for convenience's sake, shows it running
from the top edge to the bottom edge instead of the proper way,
parallel with the length of the roll.

teach a broad segment of the children in a community or just, say,
the offspring of the rich and powerful? There certainly were
schools. Not only do several of the vase-paintings described above
represent classroom scenes but schools are mentioned in Greek
writings and, what is more, in such a way as to leave the strong impression that they generally taught far more than a select few.
Greek writers considered schools worthy of notice only when
some calamity struck them; it so happens that the reports of two
such occasions, both dating in the 490s B.C., give the number of
students affected in order to underline the grievousness of the

event. Herodotus tells that once on the island of Chios "the roof collapsed on boys who were learning their letters, and out of 120 boys only one escaped." Pausanias, the Baedeker of the ancient world, tells of a famous athlete who went mad and stormed into a school in his hometown on Astypalaea, a small and unimportant island in the Aegean: "There were about 60 boys there, and he pulled down the column holding up the roof, and it came down on the boys." In an incident related by Thucydides that happened in 413 B.C., a band of bloodthirsty mercenaries descended on Mycalessus in Boeotia and, in the course of slaughtering every living creature, human and animal, "fell upon a school of boys, the biggest there, just after the boys had entered, and killed them all." Thucydides does not give the number of victims but his characterization of the unfortunate school as the "biggest there" implies the existence of at least two others—and this was in a small town in a strictly agricultural region. If schooling on this scale went on at the likes of Chios and Astypalaea and Mycalessus, why not in most other places? The instruction offered was limited very likely to the basic skills. Yet there must have been students who did not stop there. A tombstone from Athens dating 430 to 420 B.C. has a relief of a youth holding an open roll on his lap; he apparently had such a love of reading that it was recorded on his grave.

The reports about schools speak only of boys. However, since the vase-paintings mentioned above frequently picture women reading rolls, there unquestionably were literate women. Most probably they belonged to highly placed families and had been taught at home.

How many of those who could read used their ability for more than basic mundane purposes? Enough so that, not long after the beginning of the fifth B.C., the philosopher Heraclitus of Ephesus, the historian and geographer Hecataeus of Miletus, and other such savants, in addition to giving recitations of their works, committed them to writing. This meant that readers now had at their disposal prose as well as the verse of Homer and other cherished poets. A few decades later Herodotus was composing his monumental history; although he gave recitations of parts of it, its nature and

2.2 Tombstone with a relief portraying the deceased reading a roll. Circa 430–420 B.C.

length mark it as really intended for readers, not listeners. By the end of the century, reading was so common that Aristophanes could crack jokes about bookworms. He describes Euripides—a favorite butt of his—as the sort who "squeezed [his plays] out of books." In the *Frogs* he has Dionysus, god of the theater, run a contest between Aeschylus and Euripides to determine which is the better dramatist. In one trial of strength Dionysus is to "weigh" their verses to see whose are "weightier"; Aeschylus bellows that his are going to outweigh Euripides', "even if the man gets into the scale himself along with his children, his wife, and his arms full of his books."

In 405 B.C., the year the *Frogs* was presented, Euripides would have had no trouble acquiring an armful of books; by then works of all sorts were available in both prose and verse. In the case of Homer and the other classical poets multiple copies of their works must have existed because they were used in schools as reading material. "When they [the pupils] know their letters," says a speaker in a dialogue of Plato written at the beginning of the fourth century B.C., "and are getting to understand the written word, [the teachers] supply them, as they sit on the benches, the poems of the fine poets to read." He probably has small select schools in mind but, even so, no inconsiderable number of copies were required. In prose there was a multitude of handbooks on a wide range of subjects; though none have survived, we know they existed, for their titles are cited by later writers. The dramatist Sophocles wrote on that key element in Greek tragedy, the chorus, and a painter, Agatharchus, on the painting of scenery. The celebrated sculptor Polyclitus wrote an analysis of the proportions to be followed in rendering the human figure, and Ictinus, who was architect of the Parthenon, wrote an account of the building of it. And at the end of the century, or perhaps a little later, that handbook par excellence, the cookbook, makes its debut. The author, a certain Menaecus, was Sicilian, which is no surprise since Sicily's chefs enjoyed the reputation as culinary masters in ancient times that, e.g., France's do today. One prose work from the period has survived—Thucydides' magisterial study of the bitter war fought between Athens and Sparta from 431 to 404 B.C. It too, in a sense, is a handbook, on the ways of politics and the misfortunes they can produce.

Let us digress to make clear just what the word "book" meant to an ancient Greek or Roman.

The Greeks' use in Mycenaean times of clay tablets to write on was exceptional; in the centuries that followed they preferred

2.3 Sherds used in an ostracism at Athens during the fifth century B.C.
They bear the names of Themistocles and Pericles and other Athenian
statesmen of the time.

other materials. Their scratch paper was almost literally that—discarded chunks of broken pottery which they inscribed by scratching with a sharp object; they also wrote on them with pen and ink. The Greek word for such chunks was *ostraka*; ostracism, the institution devised by the Athenians whereby the citizens took a vote on whom in their midst they most wanted to get rid of and then sent the winner of this negative popularity contest into exile, was so called because the voters scratched their candidate's name on *ostraka*. For matters that called for something better than *ostraka* yet not important enough to warrant keeping as a permanent record, wax tablets were used—small framed panels of wood with one side coated with wax; the writing was easily incised on the wax with a stylus and just as easily erased by rubbing. For writings that were to be permanent, such as a marriage contract or—to come to what most concerns us—a book, the preferred material was a form of paper made from the stalks of the papyrus plant. Parchment and other prepared skins, widely used for such writings among the peoples of the Near East, did not appeal to the Greeks except to a few who shared the region and followed their neighbors' example. They did so, however, only in pre-classical times and thereafter joined their fellow-Greeks in the preference for papyrus paper.

The papyrus plant, as noted earlier, is native to Egypt and, although it is found elsewhere, only in Egypt does it grow abundantly enough to be commercially important. As far back as 3000 B.C. the Egyptians had learned to manufacture a form of paper from it. By 1100 B.C. they were exporting the paper to the Levant and, a few centuries later, to the Greek world. They never stopped exporting it and in massive quantities, for nature had given them a monopoly over it and it remained throughout antiquity the writing material par excellence of Greeks and Romans.

The manufacture of papyrus paper is relatively simple. Long thin strips sliced from freshly harvested stalks were set vertically side by side and upon these was placed a second layer of strips running horizontally. The sheet thus created was put into a press and, thanks to an adhesive quality in the natural juice of the plant, the two layers firmly cemented together to form an excellent writing material, smooth, flexible, light in color. The sheets that emerged from the press differed in size. The height was more or less determined by the length of the stalks that provided the vertical strips; these commonly varied from roughly 30 to 40 cm. Widths depended on the manufacturers' preferences and could vary even more widely, from 11 to 24 cm, but commonly ran from roughly 16 to 18 cm. The individual sheets were then made up into a long roll by being placed side by side with a slight overlap, some 20 to 25 mm, and pasted together along the overlap; for this an adhesive was needed, generally a flour paste. It was standard practice to join twenty sheets together this way. The long piece that resulted was kept rolled up for ease in handling and storing. The rolls varied considerably in length, depending upon the width and number of the sheets that went into them; a common variation was from 3.2 to 3.6 m, but there are examples that run 6 m or even more. The surface with the horizontal strips was the one primarily used to write on, so the rolling was done with this on the inside.

Writing on papyrus-paper was done with pen and ink; the ink was usually of lampblack in water, the pens of reeds sharpened to a point and split like a modern nib. A scribe commissioned to write a work on a roll would set out the text in columns, parallel to each other and extending, with room for margins, from the upper edge to the lower. After completing a column, he would roll up with his left hand and then unroll with his right to obtain space for the column to follow. Readers would handle rolls the same way, with the left hand rolling up each column after perusal and unrolling with the right to get to the next.

Someone who wanted merely to write a letter or a short document would snip off a piece of papyrus-paper of the desired size from a roll. Authors of books, on the other hand, would usually need one or more whole rolls. A play by Sophocles or Euripides would fit into a single roll of normal length, but a long work like Thucydides' history would require many. For convenience's sake the multiple rolls of long works were kept together in baskets or buckets of leather or wood.

The ancients divided up such works into long sections that they called "books." Thus the *Iliad* and the *Odyssey* consist of twenty-four books each, Herodotus' history of nine, Thucydides' history of eight, and so on. There is no connection between the number of rolls it took to hold the text of a work and the number of books it was divided into because these vary in length, often by a great deal. Book 19 of the *Iliad*, for example, with its 424 lines is less than half as long as Book 5, which has 909.

So much for what the ancient book looked like; let us return to its history. The authors of the first books to appear in Greece, around the beginning of the fifth century B.C., had but a single copy, the roll or rolls on which their manuscript was written. To convey what was in it they did what the bards had long been doing for Homer's verses: they gave readings. Thus the only people to get to know their work were those able to be there in the audience. As time went on authors met this limitation by having copies made from the manuscript to distribute among friends or other appropriate recipients, or by letting them make copies for themselves. Such was the earliest form of book production, informal and occasional.

Then, toward the end of the fifth century, a significant change took place: Greek writings of this period mention "booksellers," even a place in Athens "where books are for sale." If there were booksellers, there must have been a form of book production suffi-ciently organized and productive to furnish them with merchan-dise. They either ran or had access to scriptoria, shops staffed with scribes who turned out copies of works. We have no information about any of this, we can only guess. No doubt the scriptoria pro-duced some, perhaps most, of their copies in agreement with the authors, those who were interested in an audience larger than their circle of friends, the likes of Thucydides who expressly stated that he intended his work to be "a possession for ever." But some scriptoria owners very likely got hold of manuscripts they thought would sell and went ahead and copied them without consulting the authors; we cannot call it "pirating" since throughout ancient times such things as authors' rights, royalties, and similar matters were totally unknown.

By the beginning of the fourth century B.C. the selling of books had become a flourishing industry. Socrates, in the speech he gave at his trial in 399, remarks that the works of Anaxagoras—a philosopher who was active about thirty years earlier—"could be bought sometimes for, at most, a drachma at the *orchestra*." The *or-chestra* was a part of the agora, Athens' main square and the site where goods of all sorts were sold; booksellers obviously were so well established by Socrates' day that they had staked out their own special area. Their customers came from Athens' upper crust, people with the education to go in for reading and the money to pay out a drachma without giving it a second thought—indeed, usually more than a drachma, since Socrates implies that a drachma was the price of a cheap book, a battered second-hand set of rolls, say, or a one-roll pamphlet. Even these were not for an Athenian working man; for him a drachma could be a day's pay.

Athens' booksellers could now count on customers from over-seas. Zeno, founder of the Stoic school of philosophy, when he was a boy in his hometown on Cyprus, learned philosophy from books his father, a traveling merchant, bought for him at Athens. One of Plato's disciples had some of the master's works copied and

27

brought them to Sicily to sell; obviously there was a market there for them. As it happens, this earned him a bad name, not because he had, as it were, infringed Plato's copyright, since the concept did not exist, but because he had gone into business, the sort of thing the gentlemen of Plato's circle just didn't do.

In 405 B.C., book collecting was still so uncommon that Aristophanes could poke fun at Euripides for going in for it. A few decades later, with bookselling firmly established as a trade and thereby able to supply customers' wants, it was so no longer. Xenophon, writing in the first half of the fourth century B.C., mentions a would-be savant who had a private library that included not only much poetry and philosophy but all the works of Homer—which by itself would fill some fifteen thick rolls. A comic writer of the period even uses a private library as the setting for a scene: he has Linus, mythological master of music who taught the lyre to Heracles, usher the hero into his library, point to shelves full of works by Homer, Hesiod, writers of tragedy, writers of history, etc., and urge him to pick a copy for leisurely perusal; Heracles, who in Greek comedy is always cast as a glutton, naturally picks a cookbook.

In a word, by the latter part of the fourth century B.C., the prerequisites for the creation of the public library had been met. Works on a wide variety of subjects were available. Scriptoria had come into existence for turning out multiple copies, and there were dealers to sell them. With books easily acquired, people had begun to collect them—and become aware of how useful book collections could be. All this implies a steady increase in the number of those who were not merely literate but read for pleasure and profit.

And then, in the latter half of the century, there were two events that directly affected the first public library on record, the great foundation that the Ptolemies in the early decades of the third century B.C. set up in their capital at Alexandria.

One was the creation by Aristotle of a large personal library. Aristotle was an intellectual of vast learning and prodigious energy who produced a body of writings that covered the spectrum of the arts and sciences of his age. To aid his studies he gathered so many books that, to quote Strabo, the scholarly geographer who wrote toward the end of the first century B.C., "He was the first to have put together a collection of books and to have taught the kings in Egypt how to arrange a library." To merit such a description Aristotle's collection must have so surpassed its predecessors as to be considered the first of its kind. Its size and range were such as to require a system of organization; the one that was put in place proved suitable even for the infinitely larger collection amassed at Alexandria by the Ptolemies—for they are the "kings in Egypt" that Strabo refers to. Indeed, Aristotle's library itself almost certainly provided the inspiration for theirs. Although he died in 322 B.C. and the Ptolemaic dynasty did not begin until 305, a disciple of his, Demetrius of Phalerum, who certainly was familiar with the collection, was an intimate of the first Ptolemy and might well have suggested the creation of an enhanced version at Alexandria.

The second event was a unique decree passed by the Athenian government that bears on a key function of the sort of library that the Ptolemies aimed at attaining, namely, to serve as a repository of trustworthy copies. Even today, when books are mechanically reproduced, versions turn up that do not accurately reproduce the original. This was a far more serious problem in Greek and Roman times, since every copy was made by hand and consequently was subject not only to the gamut of errors that will inevitably occur in such a procedure but also to willful changing of the text. This decree concerns the works of Aeschylus, Sophocles, and Euripides. All plays at Athens were put on under state auspices as part of religious festivals. Within half a century after the death in 406 B.C. of the last of these three greats, their works had proven so superior to what was produced by their successors that revivals of them became the major feature of the theatrical programs. Apparently the actors performing in them took liberties with the text, so much so that Lycurgus, Athens' political leader from 338 to 325 B.C., was impelled to promulgate a law stating that:

> written versions of the tragedies of [Aeschylus, Sophocles, and Euripides] are to be preserved in the records office, and the city

clerk is to read them, for purposes of comparison, to the actors
playing the roles, and they are not to depart from them.

In other words, an authoritative version of each play was to be kept
on file, and the actors were to follow it, under penalty of law. One
of the Ptolemies, as we shall see, through deceit and vast expense
got his hands on these official versions; they represented the kind
of holdings he wanted in his library.

It is time to turn to the story of that library.

3

The Library of Alexandria

The library of Alexandria, founded around 300 B.C. or a few decades later, was the first of its kind, and throughout ancient history remained the greatest of its kind. Yet it seems to have suddenly sprung into being. Its nearest match in size, Ashurbanipal's library, was for the king's use and specialized in materials for his particular needs. The collection Aristotle put together, despite its extent and variety, was strictly personal, a tool for his multifarious studies. The library of Alexandria was comprehensive, embracing books of all sorts from everywhere, and it was public, open to anyone with fitting scholarly or literary qualifications. What caused such an institution to rise at just this time? Why in Alexandria, a city that was not much older than the library itself?

The spectacular campaign of Alexander the Great that won for him an empire stretching from his homeland in Macedon to the western border of India transformed the Greek world. Until then most Greeks had been citizens of city-states—mini-nations consisting of a city and its immediate surroundings. Each had its own politics and culture, each was focused upon itself and fiercely independent. Alexander's conquests brought an end to this. Thereafter virtually all the city-states were within one or another empire, subject to or tightly controlled by an autocratic ruler.

Alexander's death in 323 B.C. triggered a relentless struggle in the select group of Macedonians who had served as his top-ranking officers; highly capable and ruthlessly ambitious, each was out to get his hands on as much as he could of what his former commander had ruled. Soon after 300 B.C. a sort of balance had been achieved. The empire Alexander had put together had been torn into three large chunks: the dynasty of the Antigonids, with their capital in the homeland of Macedon, controlled Greece; the Seleucids, with capitals at Antioch and at Seleuceia near Babylon, controlled most of Asia Minor, Syria, and Mesopotamia; and the Ptolemies, with their capital at the city that Alexander had founded in 331 and named after himself, controlled Egypt. The period of this new world of large Greek empires is known as the Hellenistic Age; it lasted until the end of the first century B.C., by which time the Romans had finished swallowing it up.

The culture of the city-states had been insular, built on and reflecting the little worlds their citizens inhabited. The Hellenistic Age engendered a culture that spilled over narrow geographical boundaries, one more or less common to Greeks wherever they lived. The city-states had had no great funds at their disposal, only what local resources could produce; the rulers of the Hellenistic kingdoms had imperial treasuries to call upon. It was an age whose intellectual interests were inevitably broader than before—and whose rulers could afford to subsidize these interests.

In the division of the territorial swag, the Ptolemies came out best. Egypt was far richer than the lands of their rivals. For one, the fertile soil along the Nile produced bounteous harvests of grain, and grain was to the Greek and Roman world what oil is to ours; it commanded a market everywhere. For another, Egypt was the habitat par excellence of the papyrus plant, thus ensuring its rulers a monopoly on the world's prime writing material. All the Hellenistic monarchs sought to adorn their capitals with grandiose architecture and to build up a reputation for culture. The Ptolemies, able to outspend the others, took the lead. The first four members of the dynasty concentrated on Alexandria's cultural reputation, being intellectuals themselves. Ptolemy I (305–282 B.C.), was a historian, author of an authoritative account of Alexander's campaign of conquest. And he must have at least dabbled in mathematics, for it was he who, on asking Euclid whether there wasn't a shorter way to learn geometry than through *The Elements*, got the celebrated reply, "There is no royal road." Ptolemy II (282–246) was an avid zoologist, Ptolemy III (246–222) a patron of literature, Ptolemy IV (222–205) a playwright. All of them chose leading scholars and scientists as tutors for their children. It is no surprise that these men sought to make their capital the cultural center of the Greek world.

They had to start from scratch. Alexandria was a brand-new city with a population consisting mostly of soldiers and sailors of the Ptolemies' armed forces, bureaucrats and clerks of their administration, and the mixed bag of traders, businessmen, craftsman, swindlers, and whatnot, who see opportunity in, as it were, a fresh playing field. Intellectuals had to be blandished into coming to a place that to all outward appearances was a cultural wasteland. The Ptolemies offered such irresistible inducements that in the course of the third century B.C., the period of the city's cultural zenith, they were able to gather there a stellar community. From Athens, Ptolemy I got not only Euclid but also Strato, the foremost physicist of the age, and Ptolemy III got Eratosthenes, the geographer whose calculation of the circumference of the earth was astonishingly accurate. Herophilus, pioneer in the study of anatomy, after training at the renowned medical center on Cos where Hippocrates had practiced, set himself up at Alexandria. Even the great Archimedes was coaxed into leaving his native Syracuse for a short stay there.

What helped mightily in enticing intellectuals to the city was the founding by Ptolemy I of the famous Museum. In ancient times, the word museum normally referred to a religious establishment, a temple for the worship of the muses; Ptolemy's creation was a figurative temple for the muses, a place for cultivating the arts they symbolized. It was an ancient version of a think-tank: the members, consisting of noted writers, poets, scientists, and scholars, were appointed by the Ptolemies for life and enjoyed a handsome salary, tax exemption (no inconsiderable perquisite in the Ptolemaic kingdom), free lodging, and food. There was no danger of funds running out since the institution had an endowment granted by Ptolemy I when he set it up. For its quarters he turned over an area in the palace, including a room where the members could dine together. They were, in short, spared the lowly details of daily life in order to spend their time on elevated intellectual pursuits—just like their counterparts in today's think-tanks. And, as today, the members did not always agree with each other; one wag described them as

> the scribbling bookworms who are found
> in Egypt's populous nation,
> in endless debate as they flock around
> the muses' feeding station.

On top of all their personal benefits, this pampered group had at their disposal a priceless intellectual resource: it was for them that the Ptolemies founded the library of Alexandria.

It was the brainchild of Ptolemy I , even though it may not have come into being until the reign of his son. By the time of Ptolemy III, there were two libraries, the major one in the palace directly serving the members of the Museum, and a "daughter library" located in the sanctuary of the god Serapis not far from the palace. We know nothing about the physical arrangements except the negative fact that neither had a building to itself. The main library very likely consisted of a colonnade with a line-up of rooms behind, a feature common in contemporary palaces; the rooms would serve for shelving the holdings and the colonnade provide space for readers. The other library probably had a similar arrangement.

The very first problem the Ptolemies faced was acquisitions. Egypt boasted a long and distinguished culture, and there were books aplenty throughout the land—in Egyptian. There were Greek books to be bought in Athens and Rhodes and other established centers of Greek culture, but not in newly fledged Alexandria. The Ptolemies' solution was money and royal highhandedness. They sent out agents with well-filled purses and orders to buy whatever books they could, of every kind on every subject, and the older the copy the better. Older books were preferred on the grounds that, having undergone less recopying, they were that much less likely to have errors in the text. The agents followed orders so energetically that, claims one ancient authority, to fill the demand they created there arose a new industry—the forging of "old" copies. What they couldn't buy the Ptolemies commandeered: for example, they confiscated any books found on ships unloading at Alexandria; the owners were given copies (one advantage the Ptolemies did have was plenty of papyrus paper for copying), and the originals went to the library. Ptolemy III was so intent on getting his hands on Athens' official versions of the plays of Aeschylus, Sophocles, and Euripides that he was willing not only to lay out an enormous amount of money but to resort to swindling in the bargain. He asked to borrow the precious rolls to have copies made of them. The city fathers must have had suspicions, for they insisted he post a bond of fifteen talents—a huge sum, the equivalent of millions of dollars—to ensure their return. He had copies made all right, a deluxe set on papyrus paper of the finest quality—and sent these back instead of the originals. There was nothing the Athenians could do except keep the bond.

Newly acquired books were stacked in warehouses while they went through a preliminary accessions procedure. Rolls usually had a tab attached to one end bearing the author's name and ethnic. The ethnic was essential, because Greeks had only one name and, many of the names being common, different people often had the same name. At the warehouse further identification was added to the tabs to help distinguish copies of the same work from each other. Some were marked with their provenance; thus the books that had been seized on the docks were inscribed *ek ploiôn* "from the ships." Others were marked with the name of the editor or the former owner.

The policy was to acquire everything, from exalted epic poetry to humdrum cookbooks; the Ptolemies aimed to make the collection a comprehensive repository of Greek writings as well as a tool for research. They also included translations in Greek of important works in other languages. The best-known example is the Septuagint, the Greek version of the Old Testament (the name, meaning "seventy," derives, with some rounding off of the figure, from the tradition that there were seventy-two translators). Its prime purpose was to serve the Jewish community, many of whom spoke only Greek and could no longer understand the original Hebrew or Aramaic, but the enterprise was encouraged by Ptolemy II, who no doubt wanted the work in the library. The library almost certainly had a copy of the chronological list of the pharaohs that an Egyptian priest named Manetho translated from Egyptian into Greek.

Ptolemy II saw to it that special attention was given to the classics of literature—the works of the great Athenian dramatists, of Homer, and other older poets. The library became particularly strong in Homer, and for good reason: Homer was *the* poet, revered by all Greeks no matter what city or area they were from; they looked upon his epics as we do the Bible. For centuries generations had listened in rapture to bards reciting them; from the sixth century B.C. on, when the poems were finally committed to writing, they were also read and, even more important, used as schooltexts for children. But no official version had ever been created. By the time the library was amassing its collection, multitudinous copies existed with multitudinous differences in the texts they presented: omission of lines, addition of lines, transposition of lines, variation of wording, and so on. The library accordingly acquired multiple copies, distinguishing them in the ways described above, especially by provenance: it owned a copy "from Chios," another "from Argos," another "from Sinope," and so on. Such holdings made possible one of the first endeavors of Alexandrian scholarship, the establishment of a standard text for these most cherished works of Greek literature.

The rolls in the main library totaled 490,000, in the "daughter library," 42,800. This tells us nothing about the number of works or authors represented, since many rolls held more than one work and many, as in the case of Homer, were duplicates. Nor do we know what was the division in function between the two libraries. The main library, located in the palace, had to be primarily for the use of the members of the Museum. The other, in a religious sanctuary with more or less unrestricted access, may well have served a wider group of readers. Perhaps that is why its holdings were so much smaller: they were limited to works, such as the basic classics of literature, that the general public would be likely to consult.

At the head of the library was a Director appointed by the court, an intellectual luminary who often had the additional assignment of serving as tutor to the royal children. The first to hold the post was Zenodotus, famous as a pioneer in establishing a sound text of the Homeric poems. He was perforce a pioneer in library science as well, since it must have been he who set up the system the library used for shelving its holdings. We cited above Strabo's statement that Aristotle "had taught the kings in Egypt how to arrange a library"; presumably Zenodotus adapted what Aristotle had worked out for his collection to suit this much larger one. His first step must have been to sort the rolls according to the nature of their contents—verse or prose, literary or scientific, what classification of literary, what classification of scientific, and so on. The tabs gave authors' names and whatever other identification had been added during the accessions procedure but often no title; many a roll contained more than one work, and many works, such as compilations of poetry could hardly be given a simple title. When a title was lacking, Zenodotus had to unroll and pass an eye over the text. His next step was to assign rooms, or parts of rooms, to the various categories of writings that he had decided upon. And then he put the appropriate works on the shelves—arranging them by author in alphabetical order.

This brings us to one of the great contributions that we owe to the scholars at the library of Alexandria—alphabetical order as a mode of organization. So far as we know, Zenodotus was the first to have employed it, in a glossary of rare words that he compiled. Since the indications are clear that from the beginning the library's holdings were shelved alphabetically, the natural conclusion is that Zenodotus, having found the system useful for his glossary, applied it to the collection. The alphabetization went only as far as the first letter. This was the practice of all ancient scholars for all purposes for centuries; apparently such a minimal arrangement satisfied their needs. Not until the second century A.D. does fuller alphabetization make an appearance.

Zenodotus, as he put in place the library's initial organization, must have recruited the staff it required—sorters, checkers, clerks, pages, copyists, repairers, and so on. There must have been dozens of these essential employees—but we have no information at all about them, we can only surmise their existence. Like so many of the white-collar workers in the Greek and Roman world, the great majority very likely were slaves.

In the library's early years, when the holdings were relatively limited, it was enough to have a system that enabled a user to find what he was looking for by going to a given room, or to a given set of shelves in a room, and running his eye over the tabs of the rolls lined up there in rough alphabetical order. Indeed, the system was enough for inveterate users even when the library was at full strength. The story is told that Aristophanes of Byzantium, who was Director from ca. 200 to 185 B.C. and who "working daily with the utmost drive and diligence systematically read through all the books," when serving as a judge in a competition of poets held before the king, disqualified all but one on the grounds of plagiarism. Called upon by the king to prove his case, he rushed to the library and "relying just on memory, from certain bookcases produced an armful of rolls."

This bravura feat may have been possible for the likes of an Aristophanes of Byzantium, but after the collection had reached a certain size, ordinary readers needed the sort of help locating works that they enjoy today. It was supplied by a figure of towering importance not only in the history of the library of Alexandria but in the history of scholarship, a man who combined an ability to write creative poetry with a willingness to submit to the grinding drudgery of compiling hundreds of lists involving thousands of entries—Callimachus of Cyrene.

His birthplace, Cyrene, a seaport on the coast of Lybia west of Alexandria, was at the time under the rule of the Ptolemies. His family, of high rank, was in reduced circumstances. He made his way to the capital and took a job as teacher in an elementary school in a suburb there. He somehow came to the attention of Ptolemy I, who invited him to join the court's coterie of intellectuals; by Ptolemy II's reign he was its dominant figure. He may have succeeded Zenodotus as Director of the Library; if not, he certainly

3.1 Line drawing of a relief of the Roman period showing rolls, most with
identifying tabs, stacked on a shelf in three levels.

was in charge of it in some capacity, for, so far as we can tell, he was
the man responsible for its cataloguing.

As a scholar, Callimachus' greatest achievement was a monumental compilation, the *Pinakes* "Tables" or, to give it its full title,
*Tables of Persons Eminent in Every Branch of Learning together with a List
of Their Writings*. It was a detailed bibliographical survey of all
Greek writings; it filled no less than 120 books, five times as many
as Homer's *Iliad*. What made such a project possible was the existence of the library of Alexandria, on whose shelves all these writings, with rare exceptions, were to be found. And there is general
agreement that the compilation grew out of, was an expansion of,
a shelf-list of the library's holdings that Callimachus had drawn up.

The *Pinakes* has not survived; however, we have enough references to it and quotations from it in scholarly work of later centuries to provide a fair idea of its nature and extent. Callimachus
divided all Greek writers into categories—"tables," to use his terminology. These no doubt were by and large the same as the categories according to which the library's holdings were shelved and
hence were those of his shelf-list. He made an initial basic division
into poetry and prose, and broke each down into subdivisions. For
poetry there was a table of dramatic poets, with a breakdown into

a sub-table of writers of tragedy and another of writers of comedy; a table of epic poets; a table of lyric poets, and so on. For prose writers there was a table of philosophers, of orators, of historians, of writers on medicine, even a "miscellaneous table" (this is where cookbooks were listed). Each table contained names of authors in alphabetical order (by the first letter alone, of course). Each author had a brief biographical sketch that included father's name, birthplace, and sometimes a nickname—useful details for distinguishing him from other writers with the same name. Here, for example, is an entry for the famous astronomer Eudoxus which, if not exactly in Callimachus' words, derives from them:

> Eudoxus, father Aeschines, of Cnidus; astronomer, geometer, physician, legislator. He studied geometry under Archytas and medicine under Philistion of Sicily.

After the biographical sketch came a list of the author's works in alphabetical order—which in many cases must have gone on for column after column. A list of Aeschylus' plays is preserved that very likely goes back to Callimachus'; it runs to seventy-three titles. Euripides' entry must have had around that number, and Sophocles' well over a hundred. There is a list extant of the complete works of Theophrastus, the prolific savant who on Aristotle's death became head of Aristotle's school; it probably derives ultimately from Callimachus' entry and contains no fewer than 219 titles.

A key problem that confronted Callimachus was how to handle entries that involved more than one category. In the case of Aristophanes, for example, this did not arise: a writer only of comedies, he was listed on the table of such writers (no doubt up near the top since his name began with alpha). But where did Callimachus put himself, author of both prose and poetry and of different kinds of each? Did he list himself in multiple places, complete with biographical notice? Did he use cross references? We have no way of knowing.

Lists of writings of one or another kind had been drawn up before. Callimachus' "tables" were the very first to be comprehensive: he provided a systematic presentation, on one set of rolls, of all writings in Greek, literary, scientific, even functional, such as cookbooks. He was able to accomplish this because he could consult well-nigh all of them, right there in Alexandria's library. In turn, he furnished a key to the vast collection: from his *Pinakes* users could determine the existence of any particular work; from his shelf-list they could determine its location. He had created a vital reference tool.

Zenodotus and Callimachus, the dominant figures of the opening phase of Alexandrian scholarship, the first half of the third century B.C., both focused on literature. The next great figure, Eratosthenes, who served as Director from ca. 245 to 205 B.C. and dominated the second half of the century, made his mark in science. As it happens, he was learned in many other fields as well—too many, according to backbiting colleagues at the Museum, who dubbed him *Beta*, "No. 2," that is, the man who spread himself so thin over a number of areas that he was unable to be No. 1 in any single one. Not true: Eratosthenes qualified, no question about it, as *Alpha* in geography. He wrote at least two books on the subject; neither has survived but from discussions of them in later geographers we know much of what was in them. Skilled in astronomy and geometry, he enlisted both in the service of geography to determine the size of the globe and to fit the known lands on it. We have already referred to his astonishingly accurate figure for the circumference of the earth. The known lands, in his map of the world, form a vast oblong mass that stretches from the Atlantic Ocean in the west to an ocean closing off India to the east. The library's holdings not only enabled him to digest the writings of his predecessors but supplied him with fresh information on areas they had scarcely known. For India, the limit of geographical knowledge to the east, he was able to consult the accounts left by members of Alexander's expedition. For Africa's east coast, another remote area, he was able to consult the reports of the teams the Ptolemies sent down as far as Somalia to hunt elephants for the army's elephant corps.

Two noted scholars who followed Eratosthenes, both Directors of the Library, Aristophanes of Byzantium from ca. 205 to 185 B.C.

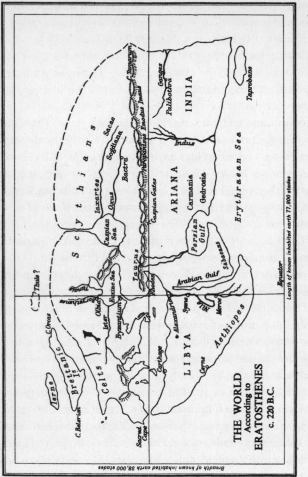

THE WORLD
According to
ERATOSTHENES
c. 220 B.C.

Breadth of known inhabited earth 38,000 stades

Length of known inhabited earth 77,800 stades

3.2 Eratosthenes' map of the world. His knowledge extended westward to the Atlantic Ocean and eastward to India.

42

and Aristarchus from ca. 175 to 145, brought the focus back to literature and language and made this half-century a golden age for research in these fields.

Zenodotus, the library's first Director, had taken the initial steps in establishing a sound text of Homer's works by comparing and analyzing the differing versions of the poems in the various copies available, much as Shakespearean experts do with the various versions in the quarto and folio editions of the plays. Aristophanes and Aristarchus carried on in greater depth and for other poets—Hesiod, Pindar, the lyric poets. And Aristarchus presented his findings in commentaries, books in which he cited given passages and then followed each passage with comments—on its meaning, on any unusual terms or expressions in it, on whether the words were genuinely the author's, and so on. He even dealt with a writer of prose, Herodotus, in this way. Such commentaries, exploited by generations of subsequent commentators, are the ancestors of today's multifarious annotated editions, from the beginning Latin student's text of Caesar to the latest "key" to Joyce's *Ulysses*.

Another area of literary scholarship that they furthered was lexicography. The rare and archaic words that turned up in Homer and the other older poets had always interested Greek intellectuals. The first formal attempt to treat them was made by a poet-scholar, Philitas, who lived around 300 B.C. He compiled a work called *Miscellaneous Words*, in which he commented, in no systematic arrangement, on a mix of such terms. It was a great success, becoming so well-known that it was as familiar to the average person as, say, Webster's Dictionary is today. Thus, in a comedy staged at least half a century after Philitas' time, there is a scene in which a host, who is planning to give a dinner party, tells how the caterer he hired discussed the menu in such fancy and archaic language that "no one on earth could understand him; . . . you'd have to get the complete works of Philitas and look up the meaning of every word." Zenodotus, following in Philitas' footsteps, made a similar compilation and introduced, as we noted earlier, the great improvement of putting the entries in alphabetical order. Aristophanes of Byzantium took the next logical step: in a work called

Lexeis, or "Words," he included words of all kinds, current as well as old, that in some way called for comment or explanation. Like so many of the scholarly products of this age, it has not survived and we know about it only through later references. Here is an extract from a glossary that, dating some four centuries after his time, perhaps ultimately goes back to his work; even if it doesn't, it is in his tradition:

> *melygion* A Scythian beverage. Glaucus, in the first book of The
> Description of Places Lying toward the Left of the Black Sea:
> "When the drivers agreed, he dismissed the assembly, and they,
> dispersing each to his own house, prepared the melygion." This
> drink is more intoxicating than wine. It is made of honey boiled
> with water, with the addition of a certain herb; for their country
> produces much honey and also beer, which they make out of
> millet.
>
> *melôdia* Obsolete term for "tragedy." See Callimachus' Commen-
> taries.

The first entry treats an unusual term, a loan-word from some language spoken in the region of the Black Sea. It starts with a succinct dictionary definition, adds—just as in our great *Oxford English Dictionary*—an example of its use, and closes with amplifying details. The second entry treats an obsolete meaning for a common term, and provides the source of the information (none other than the eminent Callimachus).

Studies in language and literature continued to be the prime concern during the last phase of scholarship at Alexandria, from the second half of the second century to 30 B.C., when Rome's occupation of Egypt brought the reign of the Ptolemies to a close. The results were summed up in the works of Didymus, so indefatigable a scholar that he turned out 3,500 books according to one authority, 4,000 according to another, and earned the nickname *Chalkenteros* "Bronze-Guts," that is, the sort of guts it took for such a prodigious output. Bronze-Guts lived during the second half of the first century B.C., toiling in the library while the western world was being torn apart by Rome's civil wars. He produced commentaries galore: on the *Iliad;* on the *Odyssey;* on the plays of the comic poets, especially those of Aristophanes; on the plays of the tragic poets, especially Sophocles; on the orations of Demosthenes. He drew up numerous glossaries, not on all words as had Aristophanes of Byzantium but on particular types: glossary to the comic poets, glossary to the tragic poets (this ran to at least twenty-eight books, longer than the *Iliad*), glossary of difficult words, glossary of metaphorical terms, glossary of words corrupted in meaning.

The first two phases of Alexandrian scholarship had produced such indispensable tools of scholarship as the authoritative text edition, the commentary, the glossary; the last phase added one more—the grammar. The author was Dionysius Thrax, "Dionysius the Thracian." He was so-called because his father had a name that sounded Thracian; actually he was a native of Alexandria, one of the few scholars treated here who was. He was a pupil of Aristarchus, and when, in a political upheaval around the middle of the second century B.C., his teacher was forced to quit the city, he left too and spent the rest of his life at Rhodes. All the scholars of Alexandria, and particularly Dionysius' teacher, had dealt in one way or another with elements and aspects of Greek grammar. Dionysius' contribution was to organize the material into a coherent whole and thereby to bring into being the first grammar book. Unlike so many of the products of Alexandrian scholarship, it has survived and we know what is in it. In a mere fifty pages Dionysius presents a succinct survey of the Greek language, starting with the letters of the alphabet and going through the various parts of speech and their forms, including the declensions of nouns and conjugations of verbs. It remained the standard grammar for Greek schoolboys for over a millennium, until the twelfth century A.D. The Romans based their Latin grammars on it, and through these it became the model for all modern grammars.

How long did the library of Alexandria last? Only until 48 B.C., when it was destroyed by fire, say some. Not at all, say others; it was merely damaged then, and not seriously.

In 50 B.C. Caesar crossed the Rubicon and precipitated the great civil war between him and his opponents headed by Pompey. Two years later, at Pharsalus in northern Greece, Caesar won a decisive victory, and Pompey fled to Alexandria. Caesar, with but a handful of ships and men, chased after him. By the time he arrived Pompey had been treacherously killed, but Caesar elected to stay on. Cleopatra, daughter of the recently deceased Ptolemy XII, was squabbling with her brother over who was to get the throne, and Caesar was interested in backing the cause of this captivating and accomplished young woman. When the Alexandrian mob was incited against the Romans, the political situation exploded into violence, and Caesar, with his meager forces, found himself in a difficult and dangerous spot. He barricaded himself in the palace area, which was near the waterfront, and at one point, to avoid the risk of "being cut off from his ships, he was forced to ward off the danger with fire, and this, spreading from the dockyards, destroyed the great library." So writes Plutarch in his life of Caesar. The historian Dio Cassius has a somewhat different version: "Many places were set on fire, with the result that, along with other buildings, the dockyards and the storehouses of grain and books, said to be great in number and of the finest, were burned." His words have been taken to mean that the destruction did not involve the whole library but was limited to books that happened to be in storehouses along the water. This is reinforced by other considerations. The bronze-gutted Didymus was active in the years after 48 B.C., and his vast and varied output would have been impossible without at least a good part of the resources of the library at his disposal. And the library was surely in existence during Antony's dalliance with Cleopatra, the years leading up to the Battle of Actium in 31 B.C. because it was rumored that Antony gave the 200,000 books in the library of Pergamum, a city within his sphere of command, as a gift to his inamorata, a gift that could only have been intended for the Alexandrian library. Plutarch, who reports the incident, comments that his source is not very trustworthy, but the story, whether true or not, could not have been told if the library had ceased to be. And there are indications that the library was in active use under subsequent Roman emperors, for there is a record of an imperial appointment of a director to it and Claudius (A.D. 41–54) built an addition to it (see Chap. 7).

The later Ptolemies, those who held the throne from the middle of the second century B.C. on, were confronted with increasing social unrest and other problems and the library no longer enjoyed the attention their predecessors had lavished on it. Indeed, some of them used the directorship as a political plum: Ptolemy VIII (145–116) gave it to an officer of the palace guard and Ptolemy IX Soter II (88–81) to one of his political supporters.

After Rome took over Egypt in 30 B.C. the emperors kept both the Museum and the library going. But membership to the Museum was now awarded, for the most part, not to men of learning but to men who had distinguished themselves in government service, in the military, even in athletics—the equivalent, in a way, of today's honorary degrees. The same possibly happened in the case of the directors of the library, if we can generalize from the one example we know about: Tiberius Claudius Balbillus, who served sometime around the middle of the first century A.D., was an administrator, government official, and military man.

The end of the library probably came in A.D. 270 or so, when the emperor Aurelian, in the course of suppressing the insurgency of the kingdom of Palmyra, engaged in bitter fighting in Alexandria. During the struggle the palace area was laid waste including, presumably, the library.

4

The Growth of Libraries

By the beginning of the second century B.C., there were other royal libraries in existence besides Alexandria's.

There was a library in the capital of the Seleucids at Antioch at least by the reign of Antiochus III (222–187 B.C.), perhaps even earlier. It was important enough to entice Euphorion, a renowned scholar-poet, into accepting Antiochus' offer of the post of director. Nothing else is recorded about it; apparently it never acquired much of a reputation.

The library that did acquire a reputation was the creation of the Attalids of Pergamum, a dynasty whose founder, Philetaerus, was a man of humble birth, a mere administrator in the employ of Lysimachus, one of Alexander's generals. In the original division of Alexander's empire, Lysimachus had been assigned Thrace, roughly what is Bulgaria and Roumania today, but, by the beginning of the third century B.C., he had managed to conquer and add to his holdings a part of Asia Minor, which included in its northwest corner the village of Pergamum. Standing atop a steep conical hill, Pergamum was a natural stronghold, and here Lysimachus stored a huge amount of the treasure he had amassed over the years, leaving Philetaerus in charge. In 282 B.C. Seleucus, Lysimachus' neighbor in Asia Minor, invaded his territory, and Philetaerus, gambling that Seleucus would win, switched allegiance. The gamble paid off: Seleucus did win, and the one-time administrator, through a combination of astute political maneuvering and luck, ended up not only owner of the treasure but also ruler of a tidy little principality consisting of Pergamum and the fertile lands about it. His successors built the principality into a flourishing empire, and Pergamum into one of the handsomest cities of Asia Minor.

The Attalids compensated for their lowly origins with highly visible patronage of the arts. They had the requirements—intelligence, taste, and, thanks to Lysimachus' treasure and the richness of the lands under their sway, plenty of money. Attalus I (241–197 B.C.), from whom the dynasty takes its name, went in for painting and sculpture. Through lavish purchases he put together an imposing collection—the first private art collection on record in the western world—and through commissions to the finest contemporary artists he adorned the city with choice sculpture. Eumenes II (197–160) continued what Attalus had begun and, in addition, turned Pergamum into a center of literature and learning by, among other moves, giving it a library that rivaled Alexandria's. Having started a century later than the Ptolemies, he had to go after acquisitions even more avidly than they had. The story is told that the people into whose hands Aristotle's noted collection had come, and who lived in Pergamene territory, buried the books in a trench to hide them and keep them from falling into the royal clutches. For the location of his library Eumenes chose an eminently fitting place: he made it an adjunct of the sanctuary of Athena, goddess of wisdom. This came to light when excavation laid bare its remains—the earliest library remains known to date.

Archaeological investigation has gone on at Pergamum for more than fifty years, through the last quarter of the nineteenth century and the first of the twentieth. It has revealed that the top of Pergamum's hill, once little more than the site of a fortress, was transformed under Attalus and his followers into an imposing civic area studded with splendid buildings. Among these was a temple to Athena. It stood within a sanctuary embraced by a colonnade, and along the north side of the colonnade excavators unearthed the foundations of four rooms in a row. These, they are convinced, belonged to the library. The westernmost is the largest, roughly 16 m long and 14 m wide, and a podium, approximately .9 m high and 1 m wide, runs parallel to its two side walls and its back wall, sepa-

4.1 Model of the Temple of Athena at Pergamum and the two-story colonnades surrounding it. The library was in the upper story at the left end of the rear colonnade.

rated from them by a space of around .5 m; about the middle of the back wall the podium widens to form a platform, 2.74 m × 1.05 m. A colossal statue of Athena was found in the temple complex and so too were some bases for busts inscribed with the names of Homer, Herodotus, and other noted literary figures. The statue of Athena, the excavators reasoned, would have stood on the platform, and the busts on the podium. A room of this size and with such decor, they further reasoned, would have served as a chamber for receptions, meetings, conferences, and so on, of the library's learned users. The other three rooms are shorter and narrower, about 13.4 m long and from 7 to 10 m in width, and these they have identified as the stacks: the walls would have been lined with wooden shelves for holding rolls. The sole indication we have of the library's size is provided by the anecdote, reported in Chapter 3, about Antony's handing over 200,000 of its books as a gift to Cleopatra; the three rooms, it has been calculated, would have had sufficient shelving space to accommodate that number. Each has a

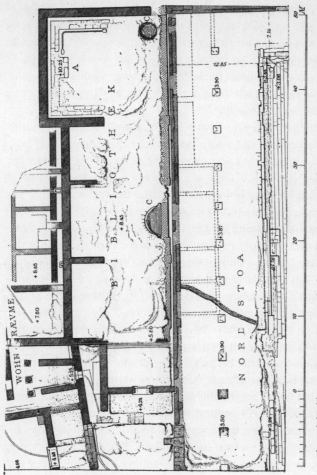

4.2 Plan of the library at Pergamum. The large chamber, A, was for receptions, meetings, etc. The line of three small chambers to its left contained the stacks. The space before the rooms, under the shelter of the colonnade, was where readers consulted the rolls.

doorway opening on to the colonnade, which would have allowed users to take the rolls out there, where there was plenty of light, for reading and study. Such an arrangement, of rooms off a colonnade, was probably modeled on Alexandria's. We know that a set of *pinakes,* tablets that listed the holdings, at some time was drawn up for Pergamum's library; these doubtless followed the pattern set for Alexandria by Callimachus.

If we can believe tales that went the rounds in later centuries, the Ptolemies were not at all pleased by the challenge on the part of an upstart dynasty to the preeminence of their famed institution. Ptolemy V (204–180 B.C.), it was said, threw Aristophanes of Byzantium into prison on the rumor that he was going off to join Eumenes in Pergamum. It was also said that "because of the rivalry about libraries between king Ptolemy and king Eumenes, Ptolemy stopped the export of papyrus, . . . and so the Pergamenes invented parchment." Since writing on leather had long been customary in the Near East, the Pergamenes could hardly have "invented parchment." What they might have done was to improve the manufacture of leather skins for writing and increasingly adopt their use, moves that could well have been triggered by the desire to reduce Pergamum's dependence on imports of Egyptian papyrus paper. There is no doubt that Pergamum under the Attalids was a center for the manufacture of such skins. Rome's supplies were so exclusively from there that the Roman word for writing-skin was *pergamena* "[paper] of Pergamum" (whence our term "parchment"). Even if embroidered, these stories of rivalry between the two dynasties must reflect a true state of affairs. Pliny the Elder, Rome's polymathic encyclopedist, had no doubts: he refers matter-of-factly to "the kings of Alexandria and Pergamum who founded libraries in keen competition." The rivalry, as the jailing of Aristophanes of Byzantium would indicate, extended to the garnering of intellectual luminaries as well, and in this the Attalids were also successful. A celebrated scholar named Crates took up residence in Pergamum and furthered the development there of a school of linguistic study and literary criticism whose theories boldly went counter to those of Alexandria's savants. And he got the jump on

Alexandria when his teachings gained adherents at Rome, the city that was soon to dominate the western world's culture. This was partly the result of a piece of bad luck that had a happy outcome. Around 168 B.C. Eumenes sent Crates to Rome on an embassy and, while walking on the Palatine hill, "he fell into an opening in a sewer and broke a leg." The happy outcome was that "during the time of his embassy and of his recovery he held an endless number of conferences and lectured constantly"—enough conferencing and lecturing to stir his listeners into practicing what he preached.

The comprehensive collections at Alexandria and Pergamum were for scholars and their like. Were there libraries of lesser rank for general readers?

One factor surely favored the growth of such libraries—a rising level of literacy. Plato, Aristotle, and other Greek thinkers had talked of the desirability of teaching all children to read and write. The Greek historian Diodorus, writing in the first century B.C., attributes to an early ruler the passage of "a law that all the sons of citizens were to learn letters, with the city contributing the teachers' salaries. For he assumed that those without means, unable to pay the fee on their own, would be deprived of noble pursuits." What Diodorus reports is more fancy than fact, but his words indicate that enlightened views about education were in the air. By Hellenistic times they had become more than just talk: there were moves to implement them.

An inscription dating to the second century B.C. that was found at Teos, a town on the coast of Asia Minor just south of Smyrna, records that a citizen left the city a sum, the income from which was to ensure "that all freeborn children receive an education." Three teachers were to be hired, one for each of the three grades of instruction offered, and the donor spelled out that the teachers "will teach boys and girls." Three teachers, even with huge classes, could hardly have handled all the children of a population that must have numbered in the thousands. But other philanthropic citizens may well have set up endowments for the same purpose; we know of this one, after all, solely because the stone on which it was inscribed happened to survive. So too has a stone recording a similar donation to the city of Miletus, south of Teos: in 200 or 199 B.C. a citizen there left a generous fund whose income was to be for the salaries of four athletic instructors and four teachers of letters. In the donor's eyes, the teachers were more important, for they were to get 25 percent greater pay. Very likely only boys were involved, since girls are not specifically mentioned. The Attalids, always eager to burnish their reputation as supporters of culture, included education among their charities. Eumenes contributed to Rhodes a huge amount of grain to convert into a fund "the interest from which was for salaries for the educators and teachers of the [citizens'] sons." His successor, Attalus II (160–139), in response to a request from the city of Delphi for help with education, gave a sum "to be an eternal gift for all time so that the teachers' salaries be regularly paid." The payment was to come from the income produced by the sum, and he even stipulated the rate of interest the administrators of the fund were to get for the money: 6.66 percent. There are a number of other places where inscriptions have been found attesting to both private and public benefactions for the support of teachers. Even the hard-fisted Ptolemies pitched in, if only to the extent of exempting teachers from certain taxes.

None of this proves the existence of anything like universal education, not even particularly wide-spread education. But it does indicate, at least for the third and second centuries B.C., a much higher level of education than ever before, and it follows that there must have been a corresponding higher level of literacy. Thanks to a special circumstance, we have proof of this in the form of masses of actual writings done by, so to speak, the man in the street.

The writings come from Egypt, and the special circumstance that made possible their survival is Egypt's climate. Papyrus paper, as we noted above, was the standard writing material of ancient times. In lands subject to normal rainfall it cannot last, since moisture destroys it. In Egypt, except for the region of the delta, there is scant rainfall, in certain places none at all, so writings on papyrus, left in pigeonholes or tossed in the trash, did not decay and vanish; they just lay where they were, gradually acquiring through the centuries a protective blanket of the country's arid sands. As a result, thousands and thousands of them, dug up by peasants or excavated by archaeologists, have been recovered, sometimes with the ink on them almost as fresh as the day they were inscribed. They are of all sorts, from the correspondence of high officials in impeccable script to scrawled laundry lists. They range in date from ca. 300 B.C. to A.D. 700, from when Ptolemy I seized Egypt, through the centuries of Ptolemaic and Roman rule, to the Arab conquest. The vast majority are in Greek, the language of the government and of the literate population.

The finds reveal how crucial literacy was to the Ptolemies' rule. The pharaohs had long exercised a comprehensive centralized control over the whole country through an organized bureaucracy of professional Egyptian scribes. The Ptolemies took over the pharaohs' machinery of government but had to create their own bureaucracy staffed by secretaries, clerks, auditors, and so on, who knew how to read and write Greek. A multitude of surviving documents relating to government matters attest to the veritable army of such personnel that must have been in their employ. And a multitude of other documents are witness to how many of the Greeks who settled in Egypt in the wake of the Ptolemies' take-over were literate, were able to handle governmental written red tape personally, able to draw up their own business papers, able to write their own letters, and the like, without having to depend upon professional scribes.

Those who were literate did not limit their reading to utilitarian ends. In a letter to a friend a resident of an Egyptian village writes: "If you have already copied the books, send them, so that we have something to help pass the time, because we have noone to talk to." There were many in Egypt like him, people who read to pass the time. We have the remains of what they read to prove it: amid the writings on papyrus that have been found, along with the government papers, the complaints to officials, the leases, the contracts, the loans, the letters, the memoranda, and so on, there have turned up remnants of literary works, sometimes even entire works. None have been discovered at Alexandria since it lies in the moist delta region, where papyri cannot survive. We can take it for granted, however, that the city, seat of the Ptolemies' bureaucracy and great cultural center, boasted as many readers as any place in the ancient world. The literary writings that have survived come from the rest of Egypt, and they reveal that the reading of books went on vigorously outside the capital, all over the land, even, as shown by the letter just cited, in villages. They reveal too what authors people read, and, if we can trust a very rough judgment based on the number of remnants found of each, what authors they liked.

Homer leads by a wide margin, with the *Iliad* favored over the *Odyssey,* preferences that held true throughout the rest of antiquity. The runner-up was Euripides. To be sure, one of the reasons for the many finds of these two is that both were used in the schoolroom, so a multitude of student copies must have existed. But there are finds that unquestionably represent copies owned by individuals, such as the beautifully written roll containing the second book of the *Iliad* that archaeologists discovered placed under the head of the mummy of a woman, or the roll with a long dramatic poem by the musician-poet Timotheus that they discovered in a coffin lying alongside the corpse. And there have turned up dozens of writings of various kinds—contemporary comedies, philosophical works, historical works, mathematical works, technical manuals, writings by obscure authors, even writings by authors hitherto unknown to us—that could only have come from personal collections.

How did owners acquire their books? Did they buy them from booksellers? Did they commission them from a scriptorium, a copying shop? Did they write them out themselves?

Homer, probably Euripides, and perhaps certain other well-known authors, quite possibly were available at bookstores in Alexandria. But copies of any others must have been written to order. There are clues that point to this. There are a number of instances in which a work of literature was written on the back of a business or government document or the like. The best explanation is that the owner of the document had kept it on file until it was no longer needed and then used the back of it for copying out the literary work. He may have done the copying himself or he may have taken it to a shop, paying for the scribe's labor but saving the cost of the writing material.

We now come to a crucial question. When a work was ordered from a shop, where did the scribes get a copy to reproduce? When an individual wanted a given book and was prepared to do the writing himself, where did he get the copy to reproduce? If the work involved was the *Iliad* or the *Odyssey* or a play by Euripides, the shop might well have a copy on its own shelves, while an individual could very likely be able to borrow a copy from a friend—or have the friend make the copy, as the writer of the letter cited above did. But what about rarer works? A copy has been found of Aristotle's *Constitution of Athens* written, in four different professional hands, on the back of four rolls that on the front contain the business records of a private estate. Clearly in this case the owner had ordered his copy from a scriptorium, supplying the paper for the job. And the shop that undertook the task might have requested access to the library at Alexandria and worked from a copy there.

But what happened when shops or individuals were in some town nowhere near Alexandria or Pergamum? Were there local libraries, or libraries in nearby cities? Libraries which, though not to be compared with great royal collections, could at least supply the works of the standard authors?

We have only straws in the wind to go by, but they are enough to indicate that quite a few cities boasted libraries. Like so many libraries today, these were supported, at least in part, by private charity, by donations from the citizens. In fact, it is because of this that we know about them: the donors were rewarded by having their names inscribed on stones that were posted prominently in a public place, and some of these stones have survived. We know, for example, that there was a library on the island of Cos, off the western coast of Asia Minor, because we have an inscription, dating to the beginning of the second century B.C., that lists men who pledged contributions to it: the part preserved records that a father and son paid for the building and, in addition, gave 100 drachmas;

four other people gave each 200 drachmas and 100 books; two others gave each 200 drachmas. The contributions in money no doubt were for buying books. Similar inscriptions attest libraries at Athens, Rhodes, and elsewhere.

All these libraries may have been connected with the local gymnasium, a feature as standard in a Greek city as its agora or theater. In the beginning and as late as the fifth century B.C. the gymnasium was just an area where athletic and military training was given to the young men of the city, the function from which the modern meaning of the term derives. By Hellenistic times it had become as well a center of learning and education, with facilities for teaching classes, holding lectures and conferences, and so on. A library would be a fitting adjunct to such an institution, and at Athens we know for sure that at least one of the gymnasiums there had a library.

This was the so-called *Ptolemaion,* in the center of town near the agora; its structures must have been a gift from one of the Ptolemies, hence the name. A series of inscriptions refer to regular donations to its library: each records that, the previous year, the *ephêboi* of Athens—a formally constituted body of young men from good families often associated with a gymnasium—had donated 100 books. One of them offers a welcome detail, that the gift included a copy of the *Iliad* and a work by Euripides; these very likely were duplicate copies or replacements for worn copies.

Another inscription, which almost certainly concerns the library of the *Ptolemaion,* is more illuminating. It is a list of authors' names followed by a varying number of titles of their works. The stone is but a part of the original, so the list is incomplete; however, enough names are preserved to make it clear that the majority of the holdings consisted of well-known writers, particularly of drama, both comedy and tragedy. Euripides is represented by more than two dozen titles, Sophocles by more than a dozen. Diphilus and Menander, two of the most celebrated writers of comedy in Hellenistic times, are represented, the first by almost a dozen titles, the second by at least three. Only two works of prose appear, one a speech by Demosthenes and the other a work by a relatively obscure essayist. The listing of the titles reveals some original arrangement in alphabetical order, which apparently got jumbled up by the time the text reached the stonecutter's hands. Euripides' works, for example, include the run: *Thyestes, Theseus, Danae, Polyis, Peliades*. It has been suggested that the inscription is a record of donations; perhaps the various batches of contributions were in alphabetical order when submitted and then suffered disorder when reduced to a single list. It is also possible that the inscription is part of a catalogue listing; if so, it was hardly user-friendly.

On Rhodes, on the other hand, a fragment of an inscription was found that is definitely part of a catalogue, and one that could well have been the work of a trained librarian. Carved on a wall, it lists authors in alphabetical order and, under each, titles of works. The first title stands alongside the name, the rest indented under the name, each on a separate line. Opposite each title, far off to the right, is a number that gives the number of books in the work. Here is an extract illustrating the arrangement:

Hegesias, *Praisers of the Athenians*
  Aspasia — one
  Alcibiades — one
Theodectes, *Art* (sc. *of Rhetoric*) — four
  On the Amphictyony — one
Theopompus, *On Sparta* — one
  On the Pan-Ionians — one
  Mausolos — one

The books were apparently catalogued by subject: the titles on this surviving piece are all of speeches or essays dealing with politics or history. Having titles inscribed on a wall was a great convenience for users: they could determine at a glance whether the collection included a work they wanted to consult, far quicker and easier than unrolling a roll—which, furthermore, would rapidly wear out from repeated use. To be sure, adding the names of new acquisitions would present a problem. Perhaps the library had a fixed set of holdings. Perhaps, inasmuch as new books did not flood in as they do today, new acquisitions, being relatively few, were recorded on a roll. The library was most likely part of a gymnasium, since another inscription, found in the same area, mentions "gymnasium officials."

In sum, what information we have, though scanty and scattered, reveals that in Hellenistic times Athens, Rhodes, and a number of other cities definitely had libraries. In Athens certainly, and in Rhodes almost certainly, the library was connected with a gymnasium. If we make the not unreasonable assumption that this was true of most gymnasiums, then there were libraries in the more than one hundred cities where gymnasiums have been attested. The libraries were supported by contributions of money and books from members of the community. At Athens, birthplace of drama, the holdings included a multitude of tragedies and comedies by well-known playwrights. At Rhodes, a noted center for rhetorical studies, the library had at least a section devoted to speeches and essays dealing with politics and history.

5

The Beginnings
Rome

Sicily and the southern part of the Italian peninsula had been settled by Greeks from the eighth century B.C. on. Through trade and travel, their highly developed culture with its convenient alphabetic system of writing became known to the various peoples to the north, above all to the Etruscans, who, from the seventh to the fourth century B.C., dominated the central part of the peninsula. The Etruscans took over the Greek alphabet and adapted it for writing Etruscan. Just south of them, and in close contact with them, lived the Romans. They took over the Etruscan alphabet and adapted it for writing Latin. Thus the Latin alphabet—the ancestor of our own—is the Greek alphabet sieved through an Etruscan intermediary.

The earliest writings in the new alphabet that have survived are mere brief inscriptions and they date from the sixth century B.C. In the succeeding centuries more extensive texts, functional in nature, make their appearance, such as priestly rituals or laws that were enacted. It is not until 240 B.C. that the first works of Latin literature enter the historical record: at a festival held that year, Livius Andronicus presented Latin renditions of a Greek comedy and a Greek tragedy.

By that date Greek literature had already seen well-nigh half a millennium of development, had been collected and preserved in the great library of Alexandria, and had been diffused throughout the Greek world. Livius reveals the massive debt that Latin literature owed to its Greek predecessor from the very outset: he was Greek by birth and his writings were translations into Latin of

Greek works. He seems to have been a native of Tarentum, one of southern Italy's biggest cities and a center of Greek culture, who was brought to Rome as a prisoner of war. There he became a slave in the household of the Livii, a family of distinction, and, when he was eventually freed, took his master's name, as was the custom. He lived until the end of the third century B.C. and produced a considerable number of translations—of Homer's *Odyssey,* of at least eight Greek tragedies, of a few Greek comedies. None of his works have survived to today, even though the Romans respectfully kept them alive long after his death. Horace, Rome's great lyric poet who wrote in the closing decades of the first century B.C., recalls how, as a schoolboy, his "whipful" schoolmaster made him learn some Livius by heart.

How did Livius get copies of the originals that he translated? There were no booksellers in the Rome of his day. A Roman who wanted a book had to send a courier to one of the Greek centers of southern Italy, where dealers were to be found; this might not pose a problem for the well-to-do but certainly would for the likes of a Livius. As we have seen, from the fourth century B.C. on, it was common in the Greek world for families with money and literary interests to have private libraries. As we shall see shortly, by the second century B.C. upper-class Romans had become passionate admirers of Greek culture: they learned the language, they immersed themselves in the literature, and they built up collections of Greek writings. Livius' career, resting solely on translations from the Greek, is a clear sign that Rome boasted such admirers already in his time, and their number would have included the family of the Livii, to judge from his connection with it. Thus the Livii might well have owned a collection of Greek classics to put at the disposal of their gifted retainer; they may even have bought copies for him.

During Livius' last years, toward the end of the third century B.C., a key figure arrives on the Roman literary scene—Plautus, the first Latin author whose works have survived. They are all Latin adaptations of Greek comedies of the type known as Greek New Comedy. These were written for the Athenian stage from about 350 to 250 B.C. and gained immediate popularity in all parts of the

Greek world. They maintained their popularity through revivals for many years after; in Plautus' day performances of Greek New Comedies were to be seen in any of the Greek centers of southern Italy.

Plautus was a native of Sarsina, a city in Umbria. Somehow he managed both to learn Greek and to acquire a masterly command of Latin. From his Greek originals he took basically the general lines of the plot and the cast of characters; the language is all his own. He employs verse forms that are far more complicated than those in the Greek and writes dialogue that is infinitely more vigorous and colorful, that sparkles with puns, alliterations, intricate word-play, striking turns of phrase. The point of all his refashioning was to hold the attention of his audiences, which consisted of the rank and file of the population. For in Rome, plays were put on as part of the entertainment at public festivals and had to compete with boxing matches, tightrope walking, gladiatorial contests, and the like. The officials in charge of a given festival would sign a contract with the manager of a troupe of actors to furnish a theatrical performance. He would buy from a writer a script, preferably of a *fabula palliata* "play in Greek cloak," that is, a Latin version of a Greek New Comedy, the type of drama the public liked best. He would then see to the costuming and props, the rehearsal of the piece, the staging. Plautus made his living by furnishing such scripts.

We know of some fifty comedies that Plautus adapted from the Greek—twenty that have come down to us and about thirty others whose names are recorded. We know the source in the case of seven of the surviving plays: six are based on works by Menander, Philemon, and Diphilus, the trio of playwrights who were the stars of Greek New Comedy, and one on a work by a certain Demophilus, who is otherwise unknown. The wide range of authorship of his Greek originals means that Plautus had access to a collection big enough to offer plenty of choice. He was not, like Livius, the protégé of a noble Roman family. He made his living by selling scripts, and they did not make him rich; indeed at times he was penniless. The story is told that three plays of his were written in his spare time from a job turning a millstone. He was reduced to this work, the very lowest form of manual labor, when he went in for some business venture and lost whatever money he had. The story is very likely exaggerated but its point is clear: Plautus was poor. Poor men were in no position to buy copies of Greek plays.

How, then, did he get texts to work from? Not from any of the families in Rome that had private libraries; Plautus, strictly a man of the theater, had no entrée to these. Even if he had, it would not have done him any good. Such collections would have consisted of the well-known classics of Greek literature with at best a few works by Menander or other popular authors of Greek New Comedy. Plautus used for his adaptations a range of plays so comprehensive that it included one by that most obscure figure, Demophilus.

Who in Rome might have had such a collection? In answering this question it will help to keep in mind a key figure in the Roman theater of Plautus' day, the manager, the combination of modern producer and director who contracted to furnish a play, paid a writer for a script, and saw to its staging. The writer probably did not even bother to keep a copy of the script for himself, for his interest in it ended when he handed it in. As Horace said of Plautus, he was "out to lay away cash in his money box, not caring whether the play stand or fall." In any event, the script didn't belong to him, it belonged to his manager. And managers indeed had good reason for keeping the scripts they bought: to use for running revivals. Thus, in the course of time, they would automatically accumulate a collection of them. Now, there is every likelihood that they accumulated as well a collection of the Greek originals used for the Latin versions. A manager made a living for himself and his company by undertaking to put on a Latin play. He entered into an agreement with a writer for a script; if no script was forthcoming he was lost. The one step he could take to ensure getting this vital necessity was to see to it that the writer had a Greek text to adapt— even better, particularly if the writer was fussy about what he adapted, a selection to choose from. Here, then, is the most likely source of the Greek originals Plautus worked from—collections in the hands of the managers he dealt with. Managers had compelling reasons to acquire texts, and they had the money to do so. They were, after all, substantial businessmen, who maintained troupes of actors and carried on negotiations with Roman officials. They could afford to send people down to booksellers in Tarentum or Syracuse to buy copies. And, to judge from the range of Plautus' output, they didn't stint in their buying.

Thus, by the closing decades of the third century B.C. and the opening decades of the second, it would seem that two types of private libraries were to be found in Rome: general collections of Greek classics owned by well-to-do families; and comprehensive collections of Latin and Greek drama owned by theater managers.

Rome's eager embrace of Greek culture, as we have noted, was already under way in the third century B.C. By the middle of the second century it was being energetically promoted by a circle of Roman nobles whose leading figure was Scipio Aemilianus. Scipio was indeed imbued with the Greek spirit: the story is told that, during the third and final war between Rome and Carthage, in 146 B.C., in which he commanded the Roman forces that broke down Carthage's last defenses and put the city to the torch, as he watched the flames rise he gave voice to his feelings at this historic moment by quoting an apt pair of lines from Homer's *Iliad*. His father, Aemilius Paulus, had brought the Macedonian empire to an end twenty-two years earlier with his victory at the Battle of Pydna. He took no booty for himself but let Scipio and another son, both "lovers of learning"—which at this time meant Greek learning— carry off the royal library.

Since speaking Greek and being familiar with Greek literature were now common ingredients in the cultural life of Rome's upper class, many a family must have put together at least a modest library consisting of the standard authors. The only collection we actually know existed was the former Macedonian library that Scipio and his brother acquired through their father. This doubtless was big and varied, for it probably had been started around the end of the fifth century B.C. by King Archelaus, who was so enamored of

Greek culture that he enticed Euripides and other Athenian literary lights into visiting the Macedonian court. And the library very likely had been enriched by Antigonus Gonatas, whose long reign (277–239 B.C.) was marked by his patronage of the arts. Scipio thus was able to offer Roman writers who enjoyed his friendship access to Greek writings outside the mainstream. Take, for example, Ennius, whom Romans considered the father of Latin literature. Among the many works he produced was a translation into Latin of the unique utopian-philosophical tale by Euhemerus about an imaginary voyage to uncharted islands in the Indian Ocean. Ennius must have gotten the Greek text of this out-of-the-way work from Scipio, for Euhemerus had spent over a decade at the Macedonian court and surely had seen to it that there were copies of his works in the royal library.

Then there were collections which we can deduce were in existence, collections not as broad as Scipio's but offering rather depth in special areas. C. Sulpicius Galus, a man Cicero regarded as "the one among the Roman nobility most devoted to the study of Greek letters," was an expert in astronomy. Just before the Battle of Pydna, Aemilius Paulus called on him to address the troops and give them the scientific explanation of an upcoming eclipse of the moon so that they would not take it as a mysterious and frightening omen; Galus subsequently wrote a book on eclipses. He must have had a library which, in addition to being well enough stocked with the standard Greek authors to enable him to earn Cicero's accolade, included the full range of Greek works on astronomy to enable him to cultivate his specialty. Galus might have gotten from Scipio the text of a well-known didactic poem on the constellations by the learned poet Aratus, because Aratus wrote it at the suggestion of Antigonus Gonatas and there would have been a copy in the Macedonian library, but this work was too elementary for a serious scholar of the subject like Galus. What he required was probably to be found only in the library of Alexandria. Presumably he ordered copies to be made and sent to Rome.

Another specialized area represented at Rome was history. This is clear from statements in Polybius. He was the Greek military and political leader who, brought to Rome as a hostage in the wake of Pydna, became an intimate friend of Scipio, lived on at Rome, and compiled a lengthy history of the Romans. This work concentrated on the fifty years from the outbreak of the second of the great wars between Rome and Carthage, the so-called Second Punic War (218–202 B.C.) in which Hannibal nearly was the victor, down to Aemilius Paulus' destruction of the Macedonian empire in 168. He wrote in Greek, since his aim was to explain to the Greek world what enabled Rome to rise so rapidly to such a peak of power. Various remarks of his indicate that he had consulted the works of numerous earlier writers. He obviously was acquainted with Timaeus' monumental history of Sicily, because, as he tells us, he continues in his introductory book from "where Timaeus left off." Others we know he went through because of the judgments he passes on them. He censures Theopompus, author of a massive history of the times of Philip II, father of Alexander the Great, for lies, acrimony, and running at the mouth. Phylarchus, who had dealt with the history of Greece in the third century B.C., he considers a writer of sensationalism rather than history. Philinus, who had dealt with the First Punic War, is too blatantly pro-Carthage. The works of Chaereas and Sosylus, which must have dealt with the Second Punic War since both men apparently had been part of Hannibal's entourage, were nothing but "gossipy chatter." He gives high marks to the memoirs of Aratus, a foremost political and military leader in the Peloponnese in the second half of the third century B.C.

Polybius thus must have assembled a collection of histories that ranged from the well-known, such as that of Timaeus, to the relatively obscure, such as those of Chaereas and Sosylus. How he got them, we have no idea. Some might have been among the holdings of Scipio and others of the nobility with whom he was intimate and he had them copied. What was not to be found at Rome he would have sought where they might be had; he traveled extensively, and this would have provided opportunities for making acquisitions. A stop at Athens, for example, could have produced a copy of Timaeus' history, for Timaeus had done his writing there, and Athens, as we have seen, was where booksellers made their first recorded appearance.

All the indications are that, by the middle of the second century B.C., there were rich library resources in the city of Rome. They were private, they were scattered, they were open to a select few— but they were there.

In the first half of the next century Rome's library resources were further enriched through wars waged in Greece and Asia Minor. War meant loot, and the opportunity to loot offered in certain places a quick way of acquiring a library. It had enabled Aemilius Paulus to bring to Rome its first library on record. It now enabled Sulla, the dominant political figure of the second decade of the century, and Lucullus, the dominant military commander of the third, to add two others.

Sulla's loot included a real prize—nothing less than Aristotle's great collection. This, as we related earlier (see Chap. 4), through the vagaries of inheritance had come into the hands of an obscure family living in the Pergamene Empire who had kept it stored underground to save it from being confiscated by the king's agents. It was eventually sold to a bibliophile, Apellicon, who brought it to Athens. In 86 B.C. Sulla seized Athens and, when Apellicon died a short time later, seized his books and carried them off to Rome. It was a literary windfall: the books included some by Aristotle and his successor, Theophrastus, that were available nowhere else. A good deal of repair was required before they could be exploited, for, during the years spent underground, dampness and worms had done considerable damage. Apellicon had had them recopied with restoration of the text where it had been eaten away, but he was a book-lover and not a scholar, and the work, done with no proper supervision, yielded copies full of errors. After Sulla's death the collection passed to his son Faustus, who seems to have taken little interest in it, leaving it in the care of a chief librarian. Tyrannio, a Greek savant living in Italy who was skilled in the handling and organization of books, managed to work his way into the man's good graces and was allowed to overhaul the holdings, and he put them into usable shape.

Lucullus' library derived from booty collected in the course of his triumphant military campaigns in northern Asia Minor. Deprived of his command in 66 B.C., he more or less left the public arena and, with the help of the vast wealth he had accumulated as a victorious general, gave himself over to a life of extravagant self-indulgence. He maintained a sumptuous town house in Rome and several equally sumptuous country villas, and he installed libraries in them stocked with the books he had brought back. The libraries apparently were laid out in the form we know from the remains at Pergamum, a complex of rooms for the holdings, colonnades where users could work, and lounges where they could meet and chat. Lucullus generously made his collections available not merely to friends and relatives but to the Greek literati living in Rome. To quote Plutarch:

> What Lucullus did about establishing a library deserves enthusiastic mention. He collected many well-written books, and his use of them was more commendable than their acquisition. He opened his libraries to everyone, and the colonnades and lounges around them were accessible without restriction to the Greeks, who would come there, as if to a reception hall of the Muses, and pass whole days together, happily staying away from their other duties.

The Greeks flocked there because the books, coming from Greek states in Asia Minor, were in their language. So too were those in Sulla's collection. No doubt as time went on some in Latin were added, but they could only have been a handful in comparison; writers of Latin had started late, less than two centuries earlier, and their total output was just a fraction of what was available in Greek.

Rome at this time also had notable libraries that were not acquired through plunder but had been put together by men devoted to literature and learning. These collections from the outset included Latin works, although inevitably the majority were Greek.

One such was Cicero's fine library. Even finer was that of his friend of long standing, Atticus, a man of great riches and learning who spoke Greek like a native. And a contemporary of theirs, Varro, to judge from the quantity and variety of his writings, probably had a library that outclassed both. Varro was Rome's rival to Alexandria's Bronze-Guts: with unflagging industry, he turned out a stream of books and monographs on all possible subjects—agriculture, the Latin language, the history of the Roman people, religion, philosophy, geography, technology. His works have almost all perished but we get an idea of the extent of the research they required from a passage in one of the few that have come down to us, his book on agriculture. Discussing who has written on the subject, he lists no less than fifty Greek authorities, whom he presumably consulted. Such research demanded an exceptionally good library.

Cicero provides us with rare and invaluable glimpses into how a Roman managed his library—or, rather, libraries, for the owners, all men of great wealth, had country villas in which they maintained collections as well as in the city. We owe the glimpses to the presence among his surviving works of hundreds of letters sent by him to relatives, colleagues, employees, friends, above all to Atticus. They are not polished missives written with an eye to publication, but informal, often casual. Cicero can leap from topic to topic, and the topics can range from doings of grave national import to the health of a child. Not infrequently there are references to books and libraries, and these reveal a striking fact: the collections he and Atticus had were so big and complicated they required organization by an expert and maintenance by a professional staff. In the Roman as in the Greek world, white-collar work, like so many other forms of labor, was done by slaves; Cicero and Atticus used highly trained Greek slaves for their library personnel. Most of them were particularly proficient in copying, since this was a major part of the work. Cicero's men, for example, turned out the copies of his writings that he distributed to friends and colleagues—and Cicero was a prolific author and had many friends. They took care, of course, of the day-to-day tasks—reshelving rolls, repairing damaged rolls, keeping the catalogue up to date, and so on.

The initial organization of a library as large and varied as Cicero's was beyond the competence of the regular staff; it called for the services of a specialist. When Cicero was installing a library in his villa at Antium (Anzio today) and the job was nearing completion, he urges Atticus to pay a visit because

> you will see Tyrannio's marvellous library arrangement of my books. . . . Could you send me a couple of your library people whom Tyrannio could use for gluing and other jobs? Tell them to bring a bit of parchment with them for labels.

Cicero had managed to get the services of Tyrannio, the expert who had put Sulla's library in order, to set up the collection; we have no information on the nature of the arrangement he introduced, but it was doubtless modeled on those of the long-established libraries at Alexandria and other Greek centers. The various routine matters that had to be tended to—for example, gluing up damaged rolls or gluing together lengths of papyrus to form rolls long enough for the copying of given works, adding strips of parchment bearing the author's name to the outer end of a roll (the equivalent of what we put on spines)—were too much for his own people, so he has to enlist extra hands from Atticus, whose holdings and staff, their correspondence makes clear, were bigger than his.

Once the books were on the shelves, one had to make sure they stayed there: Cicero was not spared that chronic affliction of library owners, theft. In autumn of 46 B.C. he writes to Publius Sulpicius, commander of the Roman armed forces in Illyria (roughly Yugoslavia today):

> My slave Dionysius, who handled my very valuable library, has stolen many of my books and, aware that he was going to get his deserts, has absconded. He is in your area. He was seen by my friend Marcus Bolanus and numerous others at Narona [on the coast of Yugoslavia, just south of Split], but he told them that I had manumitted him, and they believed it. If you could see to getting him back to me, I can't tell you how gratifying it would be.

5.1a Wall painting from Pompeii of a boy holding a roll with identifying tab.

Somewhat short of a year later, in July of 45, Cicero received a letter from P. Vatinius, the new commander in the area, who writes:

I'm told that your runaway, the reader [he was actually, as Cicero's letter shows, more like a chief librarian], has joined up with the Vardei [a people settled around Narona]. You gave me no instructions about him; however, I did issue a provisional order for his pursuit on land and sea, and I will certainly find him for you.

Vatinius was over-optimistic: six months later, in January 44, he despondently reports: "About your Dionysius; so far I have dug up

5.1b Drawing of the writing on the tab in 5.1a. It reads "Homerus."

no information." There are no further references to the matter; for all we know, the culprit may have succeeded in making his escape.

How did people carry on research in an age that had only private libraries? Cicero's letters provide answers. When he or members of his circle needed to consult books they did not own, they had recourse to each other's collections. For Cicero this usually meant tapping Atticus' ample holdings. In Rome he simply went over to Atticus' house, and he did so even when Atticus was not in residence—although he made sure of his entrée: for example, a letter to Atticus, who at the time was in Greece, includes a request that he "write home to Rome and tell your people to give me free access to your books, just as if you were here yourself." When he was at one of his country villas, which he favored for literary activity since there he was free of the pressures of the city, he would have books sent to him; in a number of letters written to Atticus from one or another of his villas, he lists titles for him to send. Or he would use the libraries in nearby villas that belonged to people he knew. When he was at his villa near Cumae, north of Naples, for example, he was able to take advantage of Sulla's library; it was in the villa not far away where Sulla had spent his final years, and Cicero was on good terms with Faustus Sulla, who had inherited villa and library. When he was at his villa in Tusculum, in the hills southeast of Rome, he used Lucullus' splendid library in a sump-

73

tuous villa close by. He was not the only one to do so: he tells how once

> when I was at my place in Tusculum and wanted to consult cer-
> tain books in young Lucullus' library, I went to his villa to get at
> them myself, as I usually did. When I arrived, I saw Marcus Cato,
> who I hadn't known was there, seated amid a pile of books on
> stoicism.

These lines come from the *De Finibus;* at the time that was written, in 45 B.C., Lucullus had long been dead, and his property had passed on to "young Lucullus." The *De Finibus* is in the form of a series of dialogues; Cicero was so taken with Lucullus' library that he made it the scene of one of them.

We know what that library probably looked like, thanks to a unique discovery made centuries ago at Herculaneum, the town Vesuvius' eruption in A.D. 79 buried under many feet of hot vol-canic mud, which on cooling solidified into rock. Excavation was begun there at the beginning of the eighteenth century, and it was carried on by hacking out deep tunnels in the rock. Toward the middle of the century, the workers came upon, and tunneled into, the remains of an elegant and richly appointed villa. They laid bare not only colonnaded courts, salons, and similar customary villa features, but also—a most welcome surprise—the villa library. This was a small chamber, approximately 3 m × 3 m, whose walls were lined with wooden shelves to above eye level, while a free-standing wooden bookcase, 1.80 m tall and fitted with shelves on both sides, took up most of the floor space, leaving just enough room for people to move freely around it. Every shelf was piled high with papyrus rolls, some 1,800 in all, a find so striking that it has given the complex its modern name, "Villa of the Papyri." A doorway opened on to an adjacent colonnade. Thus this villa library replicated on a small scale the basic elements of its great relatives at Alexandria or Pergamum: storage area for books with access to a colonnade where users could consult them.

The rolls were badly burnt and charred but enough of them could be read to reveal that the collection was highly specialized. A

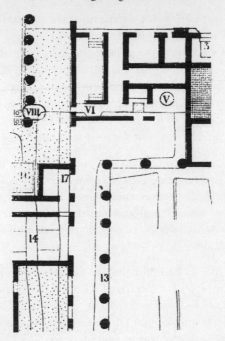

5.2 Plan of the library of the Villa of the Papyri at Herculaneum. The chamber marked V contained the stacks. Readers consulted the rolls in the nearby colonnades.

few were in Latin, all the rest in Greek, and of these the great majority were works by Philodemus, a philosopher of the Epicurean school who, from about 75 to about 40 B.C., lived in Rome or elsewhere in Italy and was friendly with a number of highly placed Romans. The villa likely belonged to one of these, a man of great wealth who was particularly interested in Epicurean philosophy as expounded by Philodemus. It has been plausibly suggested that he was Caesar's father-in-law, L. Calpurnius Piso, a powerful nobleman known to have been on intimate terms with Philodemus.

What Cato was researching at Lucullus' library involved looking into a batch of books, so he had to do his work on the spot. Had it involved merely one or two, he could have asked to borrow them; owners commonly lent books to friends or other suitable borrowers. If he needed them for extended study, he would have borrowed them just long enough for his clerks to make copies. If he needed books that were not to be found in any friend's collection, he might try to purchase them, although this had its difficulties; we will deal with the matter in a moment. At one time Cicero played with the idea of writing a work on geography, and the letters concerning it that he sent to Atticus, who was eager to cooperate, illustrate the various ways one got the books one needed. In April of 59 B.C. Cicero writes:

> I am very grateful for the copy of Serapion's book that you sent me—of which, just between ourselves, I understood hardly one word in a thousand. I've given instructions that you be paid the cash for it so that it doesn't go down in your accounts under the heading of "gifts."

Apparently Atticus had thought that Serapion's work on geography would be helpful to Cicero in his project, and, since his library holdings did not include books of that sort, bought a copy and sent it over. This was not a loan but to be kept, so Cicero insists on paying for it. Serapion was a contemporary Greek scientist who specialized in astronomy; his treatment of geography probably involved a good deal of mathematics, which would explain why Cicero, whose education was basically literary, found most of it over his head. A little later Cicero writes:

> The geographical work I had planned is really a big job. Eratosthenes, whom I had figured on using as my authority, gets sharp criticism from Serapion and Hipparchus.

He has in hand by now Eratosthenes' work, which, as the definitive study of the subject, he naturally assumed would be his primary source, and, thanks to Atticus, Serapion's. The Hipparchus he mentions was a renowned Greek astronomer of the second century B.C. who had written a book attacking Eratosthenes. Cicero presumably got Hipparchus' views from a discussion of them in Serapion; Hipparchus' own words would have been harder going for him even than Serapion's.

A few months later, in July 59 B.C., Atticus sent over as a loan a book he probably did have in his library, a geographical work in verse form by Alexander of Ephesus. Cicero didn't think much of it, but he had it copied anyway; he may have been relieved to get something on the subject that he could understand:

> I have received the book [of Alexander]. . . . He's incompetent
> as a poet and he knows nothing; however, he's of some use. I'm
> having it copied and I'll return it.

By August or September the copying had been completed, for he writes: "I am returning Alexander's book—careless fellow and a bad poet, but he has his uses." We hear nothing further about the project, so Cicero must have abandoned it; perhaps it proved too technical for his taste.

In this age of private libraries, almost all acquisitions were made, like Cicero's of the book by Alexander, through a combination of friendship and copying clerks. People acquired books that had been written in earlier ages by borrowing from friends who owned them and having their staff make copies. People acquired current books as gifts or presentation copies from the author. Those who wanted copies but did not know the author and hence were not on his list of donees, could borrow a copy from someone who was and reproduce it. Once an author had sent out his gift and presentation copies, his book was, so to speak, in the public domain, anyone could make a copy of it.

In a letter to Atticus, Cicero complains about a copy of his *De Finibus* that had been made by Caerellia, a woman who was a friend or relative of his and well known to Atticus. He was annoyed because she had made it from a copy she had somehow gotten from Atticus' library personnel before Cicero was ready to have the book officially circulate, as it were. Caerellia was "obviously aflame with enthusiasm for philosophy," he remarks with more than a touch of male sarcasm. If not "aflame with enthusiasm," she certainly was deeply interested in philosophy and, it would seem, had a collection of works on the subject, to which she was determined to add Cicero's most recent effort. Caerellia may have been exceptional as a woman owning a library but not as a woman able to exploit one. In upper-class Roman households in this age it was not unusual to find highly educated women. Cicero's daughter Tullia is described by her father as *doctissima* "extremely learned." Atticus' daughter had as tutor a most eminent teacher. Pompey's daughter was taught Greek as a child, and one of his wives not only was "well versed in literature, the lyre, and geometry" but shared Caerellia's taste for philosophy: "she was accustomed to listen to philosophic discussions." The fifty Greek authorities that Varro lists in the introduction to his work on agriculture are there as suggested reading for his wife.

It was also possible to buy books, since by now there were at least some booksellers in Rome. Cicero in one of his speeches describes an incident that took place on the steps of a *taberna libraria,* literally "book store," near the Forum. Atticus must have got the copy of Serapion that he bought for Cicero from one of the bookstores in Rome. But they were a last resort. A copy produced by one's staff from a borrowed book could be checked for accuracy— but a copy from a bookseller could not; the buyer had to take its trustworthiness on faith, and that was risky. When Cicero's brother wrote to Cicero asking his advice on acquiring books in Latin, the answer was: "For books in Latin I don't know where to go; the copies are made and sold so full of errors." Tyrannio, as mentioned above, got access to Sulla's library by ingratiating himself with the chief librarian; so did certain booksellers with the intention of making copies to sell—but their copies turned out to be of dubious value because they "used incompetent scribes and did no proofreading." When people bought books they were well advised to bring an expert along to evaluate what was offered; Cicero even tried to get Tyrannio, the expert of experts, to help his brother out.

Basically a bookstore was a scriptorium, a shop that did copying. The booksellers probably kept on hand a copy of such standard authors as Homer, Euripides, Plato, and the like, which could be swiftly reproduced for customers. They may even have maintained a small supply of copies of each to sell off the shelf. This service may be what Cicero is referring to when he writes his brother that "the books one would like to have are not the kind that are for sale." Some booksellers may have kept on hand a single copy of certain works for which there was a limited but steady demand, which they would reproduce when a customer turned up; the booksellers who went after works in Sulla's library presumably had this in mind. Venturesome booksellers possibly took orders on speculation, hoping to be able to find the requested titles somewhere and copy them.

The best place to buy books was abroad—at Athens or Rhodes or Alexandria or any of the great Greek centers where booksellers had long been plying their trade. One of Cicero's first collections came from Greece: Atticus was living in Athens at the time, and he gathered it for him, laying out the money from his own pocket. It must have been a sizable collection, for it cost more than the funds Cicero had available; he had to ask Atticus to wait to be reimbursed, assuring him that he is saving every penny for the purpose—in his words, *ego omnes meas vendemiolas eo reservo* "I am saving all my gleanings for it."

A short time before his assassination in 44 B.C., Julius Caesar made the decision "to build for public use a library of Greek books and one of Latin books, both as big as possible, and the task of building and organizing them was entrusted to Marcus Varro"—a logical choice, since Varro had written a work "On Libraries." Then came the Ides of March and with it an abrupt end to all Caesar's grand projects.

A few years later Asinius Pollio—statesman, commander, poet, historian—brought into being what Caesar had planned: a Greek and a Roman library for public use. It marks the beginning of a new age in the history of Roman libraries.

6

Libraries of the Roman Empire
The City of Rome

Julius Caesar, in the days when he "bestrode the world like a colossus," had plans to enhance Rome's cultural status by giving it a public library; his assassination cut the project short. It was revived by one of his supporters, Asinius Pollio, who was not only a respected author himself but whose circle of friends included such literary lights as Catullus and Horace and Vergil, three of Rome's greatest poets. Indeed, it was his intervention that saved Vergil's property from being confiscated during the conflicts that followed upon Caesar's death. In 39 B.C., Pollio commanded a successful military expedition and returned to Rome laden with spoils. This gave him the funds to bring into being what Caesar had brought only as far as the drawing board—Rome's first public library.

We know about Pollio's library solely through mention of it in various writings, for the structure itself has disappeared. It was centrally located just off the Forum. It had two sections, one for works in Greek and another for works in Latin, an arrangement that Caesar had planned for his library and that will appear in all subsequent Roman libraries. It was handsomely adorned with statues of famous authors, including—an unusual gesture—one of a living author, the celebrated savant Varro. Since Varro died in 27 B.C., it must have opened its doors at some point during the previous dozen years.

By this time the civil wars that had racked Rome were over or nearly so. Antony's suicide in 30 B.C. marked their end and left Augustus uncontested ruler of the Roman world. Within a few years he had laid the foundations of the Roman Empire and consolidated his position as its first emperor. He now felt free to turn his attention to matters of lesser moment, such as the condition of the city of Rome. Augustus not only saw to the repairing of the public buildings that had lain neglected or unfinished during the years of turmoil but also set about putting up new ones. Among the earliest of these, completed in 28 B.C., was a temple to Apollo on the Palatine Hill not far from the house where he lived. And, adjoining the temple, he erected Rome's second library; writings refer to it as "the Library of the Temple of Apollo" or "the Palatine Library" and reveal that it was divided into Greek and Latin sections, like Pollio's. Some years later he gave Rome a third public library, one more conveniently located in the southern part of the Campus Martius, a short walk west of the Forum. It stood in the court of a spacious, nearly square colonnade that Augustus built here that bore the name *Porticus Octaviae* in honor of his sister Octavia and was dedicated to the memory of her son who had died in 23 B.C. This library too, as we learn from references to it, was divided into a Greek section and a Latin. It has vanished without leaving a trace.

Of the library on the Palatine Hill, on the other hand, remains do exist—the earliest we have of a Roman public library. Though

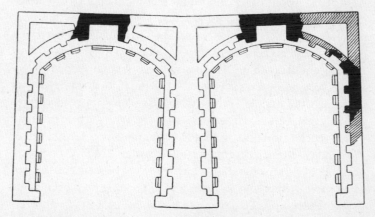

6.1 Plan of the twin libraries connected with the Temple of Apollo on the Palatine Hill, Rome.

scanty, they are all-important, for they reveal that from the beginning the architects of Roman public libraries did not follow their Greek predecessors but went their own way. Roman collections of books were necessarily bilingual; since the practice was to shelve the languages separately, the architects had to provide duplicate facilities. In the case of the Palatine Library the remains show that there were two identical chambers set side by side. In the center of the back wall in each was a large recess; it almost certainly was for a statue, probably of Apollo whose temple the library adjoined. On either side of the recess and along the side walls were niches measuring 3.80 m in height, 1.80 in width, and .60 in depth; the indications are that there were eighteen in all. Under them ran a podium which was broken by flights of steps that led up to the niches. The niches were for the books: fitted into them, as we know from illustrations and remarks in ancient writings, would have been wooden bookcases—*armaria,* as the Romans called them—lined with shelves and closed by doors. The bookcases would have been numbered and the appropriate number entered in the catalogue alongside each title to indicate the location. The rolls of the library's collection would have been laid horizontally on the shelves with the ends bearing the tag of identification facing outward. Thus, when users climbed the steps and opened the doors, the tags would have been immediately visible to them. Since the niches were so high that their upper shelves would have been well beyond a man's reach, there must have been portable sets of steps available on the podium, like those we use in libraries today to get at books on the topmost shelves. The placing of the holdings in wall niches left the middle of the chamber available for readers; presumably tables and chairs were set up here. With such an arrangement—books along the walls and accommodation for readers in the middle—Roman libraries were like modern reading rooms and not at all like Greek libraries, which, as we have seen, consisted of small rooms, where books were stored, opening on a colonnade, where readers consulted them. In a way, users of the Palatine Library had the best of both worlds: because the colonnade that surrounded the temple of Apollo was nearby, they could, if they wished, take the books out there, just as in a Greek library.

This layout for a library was a Roman innovation. Had it been part of Caesar's design? Was it Pollio's idea? Or does the credit go to Augustus, his Palatine Library being not merely the first evidence for it but the first example of it? We have no way of knowing.

Until Augustus' death in A.D. 14, Rome had only these three public libraries: Pollio's next to the Forum; the one in the Porticus

6.2 Physician reading a roll. Alongside is a bookcase fitted with doors; on the first shelf is a stack of rolls, on the second what may be a cup used for bleeding. On the top of the bookcase is his instrument case.

of Octavia, an easy walk from the Forum; and Augustus' on the Palatine hill, conveniently located for himself and members of his circle. The next emperor, Tiberius, sometime during his reign (14–37) added another, perhaps two, on the Palatine Hill, and Vespasian added yet one more as part of the Temple of Peace that he erected near the Forum after the end of the Jewish War in A.D. 70. No remains can with certainty be attributed to Tiberius' library. Some have been attributed to Vespasian's, but hardly with certainty and, in any event, they are too fragmentary to offer much information. Tiberius' library must have been sizable, for we are told that it was decorated by a statue of Apollo almost fifty feet high; this would have stood in a recess in the back wall, as in the Palatine Library, and a chamber boasting a recess for such a colossus would easily have been high enough to accommodate two superimposed rows of niches for bookcases, a feature that is attested in a number of later libraries.

Finally we come to a library that offers more than a scattering of remains—the library included by the emperor Trajan as part of the monumental forum he dedicated in A.D. 112/113. Enough of it survives to make possible an almost complete reconstruction of its interior.

The Forum of Trajan extends more or less alongside the Capitoline Hill; between it and the hill runs the modern boulevard called the Via dei Fori Imperiali. The noted Roman tourist attraction, Trajan's Column, belongs to this complex, and only a short distance from the column are the remains of the library; they are, however,

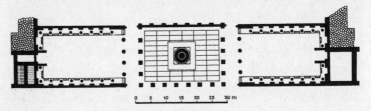

6.3 Plan of the twin libraries of the Forum of Trajan, Rome. They face each other with the Column of Trajan and the portico surrounding it between them.

invisible to today's sightseers because they have been covered over by the paving of the boulevard. There was, as usual, a pair of chambers, one for Greek works and one for Latin. In the Palatine Library the two were side by side; here they faced each other, being on opposite sides of a square portico in whose center stood Trajan's Column. Readers who needed to consult books in both languages had to walk some 40 meters from the entrance of one, past the portico with its column, to the entrance of the other. The chamber on the side toward the Capitoline Hill, that is, to the southwest of the column, is well preserved: its remains, though they lie beneath the Via dei Fori Imperiali, are accessible, for they are in an underground pocket roofed by beams that support the boulevard's paving. They include the floor, lower portions of the walls, and a multitude of fragments of marble and stone that come from elements of the decoration. The remnants of the other chamber are few but enough to reveal that it was a twin.

The chamber we can reconstruct, the southwest chamber, was spacious, measuring 27.10 m along its sides and 20.10 along the front and back. It was airy as well, for it rose two stories high and was covered by a vaulted roof, probably of cross-vaults. The wall forming the back of the chamber had in its center a recess big enough to accommodate an oversize statue; on either side of the recess were an upper and a lower level of niches for bookcases, two per level. The walls forming the sides of the chamber had each an upper and a lower level of seven niches. Under the lower level ran a podium, broken in front of each niche by a flight of three steps to give access to the books it held. The upper-level niches have been lost but there are sure indications of their existence, notably a row of columns set on the podium and spaced so that each was opposite the interval between one niche and the next; they were there to support a gallery that served this upper level. A staircase at the back of the building provided access to the gallery. The front side of the chamber, that facing Trajan's Column and the twin chamber beyond it, was open; there was no wall here, just four columns topped by an entablature. This side served as the entrance; the absence of a wall meant there could be no doors, so, between the

6.4 Reconstruction of the interior of the southwest library of the Forum of Trajan, Rome.

columns were set bronze screens which were closed when the library was not in use. Facing northeast, the entrance caught the morning light; windows on the other three sides in the semicircles formed by the vaults of the roof ensured light the rest of the day.

The decoration of the chamber was sumptuous; Trajan had al-

6.5 Reconstruction of the front of the southwest library of the Forum of Trajan showing the four columns that marked the entrance and the movable bronze grills that spanned the spaces between them, thereby permitting the closing of access to the chamber during off-hours.

lowed his builders lavish use of marble and stone, much of it imported. The floor was paved with large rectangles of gray granite from Egypt separated by strips of yellow marble from north Africa. The construction material of the walls, brick-faced concrete, was everywhere covered with a veneer of pavonazzetto, a marble of variegated colors from Asia Minor. Each niche was framed in white marble and topped by a cornice of white marble. The columns supporting the gallery were of pavonazzetto, with bases and capitals of white marble. They stood opposite pilasters of pavonazzetto that decorated the wall space between niches. The statue in the recess was of white marble, probably an image of the man responsible for it all, books as well as building, the emperor Trajan.

The niches in the side walls have a width of 1.61 m, while those flanking the recess at the back, with a width of 1.35, are somewhat narrower. Since only the lower portions have been preserved, we must estimate the height: a good guess is that it was double the width, that is, 3.23 m. The depth is .625 m. The marble frame that surrounded the niches projected beyond their edges on all four sides; this ensured that space was left between the sides of the niches and the wooden bookcases inserted in them. There was space left behind as well, for the niches were .625 m in depth and the bookcases, made to accommodate rolls whose maximum height rarely went beyond .40 m, would be considerably less deep. As a result, the bookcases nowhere made contact with the wall, thereby insulating the rolls they held, which were susceptible to moisture, from dampness in the walls. With an upper and lower set of seven on each side wall and of four on the back wall, there was a total of 36 bookcases. Their capacity, it has been estimated, was some 10,000 rolls. If we double the figure to include what was in the sister chamber, the collection in Trajan's library numbered in the neighborhood of 20,000.

The detail furnished by Trajan's library reveals dramatically the vast difference between Greek and Roman libraries. Greek libraries were, in essence, stacks. No facilities were supplied for readers; they were left to work in a contiguous colonnade, which was a part of the complex the library was in, not of the library itself. A Roman library was just the opposite: it was designed primarily for readers, to provide them with spacious, handsome surroundings in which to work. The books themselves were nearby yet out of the way, on shelves within the walls. Such a room, with its handsome niches tastefully disposed and very likely embellished by bookcase doors of precious woods artistically carved, was immensely pleasing to the eye but recklessly wasteful of space, a factor that was bound to create problems as collections grew.

The imperial public libraries described so far were, like Augustus' on the Palatine Hill, attached to a temple or, like that in the Forum of Trajan, within a large complex. They were not an integral part of these, however; they were independent of them, their sole function was to serve those who came to consult the books they held. No doubt most of their users were people with a professional interest in, or deep-seated feeling for, literature and learning—

writers, lawyers, philosophers, teachers, scholars, and the like. No doubt these users represented but a tiny fraction of Rome's total population. Yet their actual number could well have been considerable, for the city's renown as one of the great cultural centers and as the center par excellence for Latin studies must have drawn their like from all over.

Trajan's was the last of such libraries to go up. This does not mean that construction of public libraries in Rome came to an end. It went on, but in a special place where the libraries clearly served a wider and different audience: they were incorporated in the imperial public baths.

As early as the second century B.C. public baths existed in Rome, and they became so popular that by the middle of the next century there were almost two hundred of them. But only people with money could use them: they were all privately owned and charged a fee. This limitation was removed when the citizens of Rome, in addition to the free "bread and circuses" that they had long enjoyed, were given by Augustus' minister Agrippa a set of baths that were free. Subsequent emperors went a step further: they built baths that were not only free but superbly equipped and sumptuously decorated. What is more, over and above offering the full range of services of a bathing establishment—warm rooms, hot rooms, sweat rooms, cold plunges, massage chambers, and so on— these complexes served as recreational and cultural centers: surrounding the central core that housed the bathing facilities were gardens with paths for walking, courts for exercising or playing games, rooms for meetings or recitals or lectures—and libraries.

The first of the grand imperial baths was put up by Nero; as a Roman satirist quipped, "What worse than Nero? What better than his baths?" Only insignificant ruins from it are visible today. The first of which enough survives to give us some idea of their size and splendor are the Baths of Trajan, completed in A.D. 109. The remains are far from complete but luckily they include portions of the library.

There were the usual two chambers. Each was accommodated in a shallow apse in the wall that fenced off the huge complex, one

6.6 Remains of the library of the Baths of Trajan, Rome.

in the wall along the western side and the other opposite it far off in the wall along the eastern. Readers who wanted to consult books in both Greek and Latin had a walk of over a fifth of a mile, some 300 meters. The apse in the western wall is well enough preserved to show that the basic features were like those in the library of Trajan's Forum: in the center of the curved wall that formed the back of the area was a large niche for a statue; on either side were niches for the bookcases—two rows, one above the other, of five niches each, twenty in all. The niches, measuring 4.45 m in height, 2.06 in width, and .73 in depth, are considerably bigger than those in the Palatine library or the library of Trajan's Forum.

Even better preserved is the library of one of Rome's famed sights, the Baths of Caracalla, begun in A.D. 212 but not completed until a decade or more later. As in Trajan's baths, there are two chambers set in the enclosure wall, in this case some 260 meters apart at the southwest and southeast corners of the complex. The library areas in Trajan's baths were apsidal; here they were rectangles measuring 36.3 m by 21.9 m. The long sides formed the front and back of the chamber. The front opened on a colonnade that ran along before it—literally opened on the colonnade because this

6.7 Remains of the library of the Baths of Caracalla, Rome.

side had no wall, just a row of ten columns. Users left the colonnade and passed through the columns to enter the chamber. Very likely there were bronze screens between the columns, as in the library of the Forum of Trajan, to close the library during off-hours. In the center of the back wall was the usual recess, which, to judge from its breadth and height, must have accommodated a statue of colossal size. In the space on either side of the recess, and along the short walls, were the niches for the bookcases, two superimposed rows of them, three per row on each side of the recess and five per row on each side wall, making a total of thirty-two. Under the lower row ran a podium broken by steps in front of each niche; on it stood the columns that supported a gallery serving the upper level.

Big as the Baths of Caracalla were, an even bigger set was put up in A.D. 305–6 by Diocletian. There probably was a library, but we cannot be sure and may never be, because it would be part of the unexcavated portions of the complex and these lie under modern buildings and streets.

The public baths were patronized by all Romans, men and women, young and old, rich and poor. They came there not only for the bathing facilities but to pass time in leisurely activities, to walk in the gardens, play ball or watch others play ball, listen to lectures, chat with friends—or browse in the library. The contents of the bath libraries must have reflected this state of affairs, namely that the readership would consist primarily of people who turned to the books there as a pastime, as an alternative to tossing a ball or indulging in casual conversation, and only secondarily of professionals and literati who found it convenient to combine a bath with some study. Presumably the collections emphasized well-known classics and had numerous copies of Homer and Euripides and Menander in the Greek section, of Ennius and Plautus and Vergil in the Latin, and few of, say, philosophers in either.

The emperors cared deeply about Rome's public libraries. From Augustus to Trajan, they steadily increased their number. From Trajan on, perhaps even earlier, they added libraries as part of the public baths and continued to do so at least until the beginning of the third century. They saw to it that the libraries they built remained in use. When the Palatine Library was wiped out in the great fire of A.D. 64 (the one Nero purportedly fiddled to), it was restored in Domitian's reign (81–96). When the library in the Porticus of Octavia burned down in A.D. 80, Domitian rebuilt it and went to the trouble of replacing some of the lost holdings with copies from Alexandria. In 191, fire destroyed Vespasian's Temple of Peace and presumably the library with it, but complete restoration must have been carried out because the temple was one of the city's sights in 357. A catalogue of Rome's noteworthy buildings dating about 350 indicates that there were at that time twenty-nine libraries in the city, a figure that unquestionably includes some, if not all, of the imperial libraries. Trajan's library was still standing in 456, because a speaker who delivered a panegyric to the emperor that year is able to boast that his reward was having his statue placed amid those of the authors that graced it.

So much for the bricks and mortar of Rome's libraries. Let us turn to the personnel that ran them.

Pollio and Augustus began their libraries from scratch: they had to determine the nature of the collection, acquire the books, decide how to arrange them, catalogue them, and so on. Pollio, a man of letters with, no doubt, a large personal library, may have taken care of all this himself; he may even have donated books of his own to his new creation or at least have had them copied for it. Augustus, immersed in war and politics from Caesar's death in 44 B.C. to shortly before he opened his first library, had none of these advantages; he had to seek professional help. The task of setting up the Palatine Library he entrusted to Gnaeus Pompeius Macer. Macer's father was a distinguished Greek statesman who was also an historian; becoming a close friend of Pompey the Great, he wrote a history of his campaigns, and a grateful Pompey awarded him Roman citizenship. The son stood high in Roman government circles, and we can only assume that, like his father, he had intellectual and literary credentials, enough to have gained him the assignment. The library in the Porticus of Octavia Augustus turned over to Gaius Maecenas Melissus. Socially Melissus was Macer's opposite: he started life as a slave, somehow received an education, came into the hands of Maecenas, the patron of Vergil and Horace and Augustus' advisor on matters of culture, was manumitted by Maecenas, and introduced by him to Augustus. Melissus was a respected scholar and author of works ranging from plays of a novel type to a comprehensive collection of jokes. He was a natural choice to handle the setting up of a library.

Once these men had selected the titles they wanted and seen to their acquisition, cataloguing, and arranging, their job was done. What happened next we know in the case of the Palatine Library: Augustus appointed a permanent head, Caius Iulius Hyginus, an eminently qualified freedman like Melissus. Hyginus had studied under a renowned teacher, had become a renowned teacher himself, and had written numerous scholarly studies. Presumably Augustus appointed a similar learned freedman to head the library of the Porticus of Octavia.

Our information about Macer, Melissus, and Hyginus comes from ancient authors, in particular Suetonius, who lived in the early second century and who wrote biographies of distinguished men of letters as well as the biographies of Roman emperors for which he is famous. Our information about the next figures connected with Rome's libraries comes almost wholly from surviving inscriptions on stones, specifically epitaphs and honorary decrees. Roman epitaphs commonly tell what the deceased did in life—in

the case of the humble their occupations, in the case of the elevated their government posts. Honorary decrees, which by their
nature involve only the elevated, spell out the various stages in the
honoree's career.

Through epitaphs we know of two library officials who served
during the reigns of Tiberius, Caligula, and Claudius, that is, during
the years between A.D. 14 and 54. An expensive tombstone—it is
of white marble, made in the form of an altar, and decorated with
sculpture—memorializes Tiberius Julius Pappus, who "was an
intimate of Tiberius and likewise in charge of all the libraries of
the emperors from Tiberius Caesar to Claudius Caesar." Another
tombstone, this one spare and simple, memorializes "Tiberius
Claudius Scirtus, freedman of Augustus, Director of the Libraries;"
the term "freedman of Augustus" is the designation of one who, of
slave origin, had come into the emperor's possession and been
manumitted by him. The two inscriptions reveal that Tiberius had
created a new post, administrator of all Rome's libraries, and Scirtus' gravestone supplies the official title, "Director of the Libraries"
(*procurator bibliothecarum*). If we assume, as is quite likely, that Pollio's library had come under imperial supervision, Tiberius had
four, perhaps five, public libraries on his hands, and he apparently
thought that this many called for a centralized management. The
inscriptions further reveal that, if not both, certainly one of the appointees was, like Hyginus, a freedman—but a freedman of a very
different type from Hyginus. Scirtus was not a scholar or writer; he
was a bureaucrat who achieved the post in the course of a career in
the imperial service.

We mentioned earlier that the Romans left most white-collar
work to slaves and freedmen. This was true of state as well as private employees. One of Augustus' moves to improve his government's efficiency was to set up an organized bureaucracy, which he
staffed with slaves belonging to the imperial household. The able
among them, as they advanced in age and position, gained manu-
mission and continued to carry on their duties as freedmen. These
slaves and freedmen of the emperor, the so-called "family of Caesar" (*familia Caesaris*), ran the gamut of employment from lowly

clerk in the most minor of departments to head of the highest; they were, in effect, a civil service. They spent their lifetime in it, with the ambitious climbing the ladder of promotion. The office of procurator was near the top; indeed, the procuratorship of a major department could be the very top. Scirtus was a successful member of this bureaucracy, a man who had arrived at a not unimportant procuratorship. He almost certainly did not have the literary or scholarly qualifications of a Hyginus, but this would have been no drawback because the work was primarily financial and managerial: reviewing the budget, purchasing supplies, making sure the libraries were operating smoothly, and so on. Pappus and Scirtus died while in office, probably after holding it for years; indeed, Pappus' incumbency spanned the reigns of three emperors. This could have been of benefit both to him and the library staffs under him. He had the time to familiarize himself thoroughly with the job, and they were spared the disruption that frequent turnover in the headship might have caused.

The next Director of the Libraries that we know of is Dionysius of Alexandria, and he reflects a shift that the emperors from Vespasian (A.D. 69–79) on introduced in the manning of government posts: for the higher levels they turned to freeborn men of the upper economic and social class. Dionysius was no ex-slave; he was a distinguished Greek, citizen of Alexandria, and a scholar whose stature carried him appointment as head of the Alexandrian Museum. He probably entered government service under Vespasian or Titus (79–81). His first post was the directorship of the libraries and then he became Secretary of Greek Affairs. Dionysius' background obviously made him a fitting choice to head up a group of libraries. But since it was an office he took on as part of a career, he must have held it for a limited time, giving it up when he moved on to the next higher, his secretaryship. In other words, the Director of the Libraries no longer served for an extended period, as he had when the position could be the culmination of an imperial freedman's lifetime in the bureaucracy.

The names and careers of almost half a dozen Directors of the Library under Hadrian (117–138) and Antoninus Pius (138–161)

are known, and they show the expansion of what was just beginning at the time of Dionysius' appointment: they are all men from
the upper levels of the freeborn who spent their lives in government service, steadily rising in the administrative ranks. The Directorship of the Libraries, although it paid a good salary, was but a
rung of the ladder, and a relatively low one at that. Here, for example, is the *curriculum vitae* of Valerius Eudaemon, who owed most of
his advancement to Hadrian:

> Commissioner of Finance at Alexandria; Director of the Libraries,
> both Greek and Latin; Secretary of Correspondence in Greek;
> Procurator of Lycia [followed by the procuratorship of six other
> regions of Asia Minor]; Commissioner of Inheritances; Procura-
> tor of the Province of Asia; Procurator of the Province of Syria;
> Praefect of Egypt.

Eudaemon entered government service at an advanced level, skip-
ping a number of army ranks that at the time it was customary to
hold first. Once in it, he reached the top, for Praefect (Governor) of
Egypt was the highest a man of his social standing—that is, not a
member of the aristocracy—could normally aspire to. Eudaemon
must have brought to his term as Director of the Libraries financial
and administrative expertise, but, in view of his crowded career,
the libraries could not have enjoyed the benefits of that expertise
for any great length of time. Though there is no indication in his
record of scholarly or literary attainments, he may very well have
had some, since most of the other appointees to the post whom
we know of did. One was a philosopher, another was a jurist, yet
another was Suetonius—who might well have garnered during his
term in office the information he supplies us about Macer, Melissus, and Hyginus along with other matters connected with Rome's
libraries.

Thus, from the time of Vespasian to at least the middle of the
second century A.D. and quite possibly later, the running of Rome's
libraries was in the hands of men for whom the position was a step-
ping stone to higher office and who gained it by demonstrating
ability as government servants plus, no doubt, skill in getting into

an emperor's good graces. Unlike their predecessors, it was for them much closer to the bottom of the ladder than the top. On the other hand, as the example of Dionysius and Suetonius and others shows, they brought to the office familiarity with the world of learning and literature; they were themselves users of libraries. The staffs of the libraries may have lost the benefits of a long-term relationship with their head that they enjoyed in the days of freedman officials, but they gained in having over them men fitted to deal with the collections as well as the budget.

The staffs themselves consisted of slaves and a sprinkling of freedmen. In the libraries created by the emperors they came from the *familia Caesaris*, and no doubt in Pollio's as well, once it had passed under imperial supervision. At the head of each staff was a *bibliothecarius* "librarian." That this was his title emerges from a jocular passage in a letter sent in 144/145 by Marcus Aurelius, the future emperor (161–180), to his teacher, Fronto. Aurelius writes that he has just read two very interesting books, he is sure Fronto will want to read them, but Fronto shouldn't go after the copies in the library of the Temple of Apollo, since he (Aurelius) has those, he should try blandishing the *bibliothecarius Tiberianus* "the librarian of Tiberius' (library)."

The *bibliothecarius* had under him a group of employees who, as we know from epitaphs on their or their family's gravestones, were mostly classified simply as *a bibliotheca* "of the library staff" plus indication to which library and which section of it, Latin or Greek, they belonged. For example:

Antiochus, [slave of] Tiberius Claudius Caesar, of the staff of the Latin library of the [temple] of Apollo.

Laryx, of the staff of the Greek library of the Porticus of Octavia.

A few gravestones are slightly more specific:

Montanus Iulianus, *vilicus* of the Latin library of [the Porticus of] Octavia.

Onesimus, [slave of] Caesar, *vilicus* of the Greek library of the baths.

The term *vilicus* means "steward"; perhaps he took care of maintenance of the building, while those referred to as "of the library staff" dealt with the books—the pages who fetched rolls from the bookcases and returned them there, the restorers who mended torn rolls, above all the scribes. Scribes must have made up the biggest part of the staff, since there was a whole range of time-consuming duties they had to perform: making copies to add to the collection, recopying damaged rolls, keeping up the catalogue, and so on. Whether pages or conservators or scribes, literacy was essential, and this explains why the men were assigned to either the Greek or Latin section; it depended on their language skill.

One gravestone is unusual. It was put up by:

> Tiberius Claudius Hymenaeus, freedman of Augustus, physician
> for the libraries (*medicus bibliothecis*).

Hymenaeus' social status was higher than the others: he was a freedman, not a slave. Moreover, he was not attached to any one library but served the whole complex. There were enough people in the library staffs, it would seem, to justify their having their own doctor, and the emperor was concerned enough to supply one.

To sum up, Rome's libraries were under a Director of the Libraries (*procurator bibliothecarum*) who dealt with the financial and managerial affairs of the group as a whole; from the reign of Tiberius to Vespasian he could be a freedman from the imperial civil service (*Augusti libertus* aut sim.), from Vespasian on he was freeborn from the upper levels of society. Each library had a staff made up of slaves of the imperial civil service (*Caesaris servi* aut sim.). The staff was headed by a Librarian (*bibliothecarius*). Under him were subordinates, assigned specifically to the Greek or Latin section of his library and called "of the library staff" (*a bibliotheca*); most of the staff were probably scribes.

What was the make-up of the collections that these staffs took care of?

So far as Greek titles are concerned, Rome's libraries must have been ruthlessly selective. The library at Alexandria, intended to serve as a comprehensive repository of Greek writings, had 490,000 rolls. Its rival at Pergamum had at least 200,000. The library of the Forum of Trajan, quite likely Rome's largest, had space for but 10,000 in its Greek chamber. The Palatine Library, with half as many bookcases, held far fewer. There is no reason to think that Tiberius' and Vespasian's were markedly bigger. In other words, the Greek holdings in Rome's public libraries were a fraction of what was available.

Latin, however, was a different matter. When Pollio opened the first public library, though he was confronted by some seven centuries of writings to choose from for his Greek section, he had but two to deal with for his Latin. Conceivably he had space for all that he considered worthwhile.

We have only haphazard indications as to what books his or the other libraries had on their shelves. For example, the knowledge that the three in existence at the time of Augustus all included contemporary authors in their holdings we owe to a misfortune that befell the poet Ovid. One of the leading literary lights at the court of Augustus, he got involved in some scandal, and in A.D. 8 he was banished from Rome and his books blacklisted. This elicited from him the lament, in a poem he wrote while in exile, that the Palatine Library "offers readers the works of men of learning of both the past and the present" but has none of his, nor does the library of the Porticus of Octavia or Pollio's. In other words, the Palatine Library stocked both earlier and contemporary writing and the other two stocked at least contemporary work such as Ovid's poetry. We mentioned earlier that Pollio put a statue of Varro in his library while Varro was still living; it is a reasonable inference that the collection included Varro's voluminous output. We can deduce from a remark in Suetonius' biography of Caligula that all the libraries in his day had the works of Vergil and Livy, for Suetonius reports that Caligula took such a dim view of these two authors "he came close to banning their writings and statues from all the libraries."

Roman libraries, with a limited capacity to begin with, of which much would be taken up by a representative selection of older works, as year after year they added contemporary Latin writings would sooner or later run out of space. Modern libraries, when confronted with this problem, find room somewhere to put up more shelves. For Roman libraries, with their handsome bookcases set in niches carefully arranged along the walls of a single chamber, that solution was unlikely.

One way to meet the problem was to build more libraries, and this may well be the reason why the number increased steadily right up to Trajan's reign, or even beyond if we include libraries in baths.

Another way, resorted to by many libraries today, is creation of separate storage areas for books infrequently used. There is an anecdote in Suetonius' biography of Caesar which perhaps indicates that Roman librarians may have taken this path. Discussing Caesar's writings, Suetonius remarks that Augustus "sent a short and direct letter to Pompeius Macer, whom he had put in charge of arranging the [Palatine] library, forbidding him to let circulate" certain pieces Julius Caesar had written as a youth. Suetonius' language implies that Augustus, who no doubt was embarrassed by the juvenile effusions of his revered relative, wanted them merely out of sight, not destroyed. Nor were they destroyed, for Suetonius, writing a century and a half later, lists their titles and thus must have had access to them. It sounds as if they were put in storage—and so might other writings which, like them, were of dubious quality but had some claim to being saved.

There is yet another possibility: when it became clear in the course of time that space was going to run short, the libraries may have resorted to specialization, may have assigned each a field on which to concentrate. Consider their geographical location. They were not scattered about, as they would be if their purpose was to make available well-rounded collections to readers in different locales. The two on the Palatine Hill no doubt were for the use of the emperor and his circle. The other four were clustered around the Forum; save for reference books or standard works, there was no reason for all of them to stock the same titles. It would make sense for each to offer depth in a given area; readers whose studies involved several areas could easily walk from one to the other.

One person thoroughly familiar with Rome's public libraries was Aulus Gellius, who lived in the second century, when they had long been in existence and the nature of their holdings well established. Gellius was a haunter of bookstores and libraries; he devoted his life to the study of literature and language, immersing himself in questions of usage, meaning, grammatical forms, and the like. His lengthy book, *Attic Nights*, is full of information on such matters, and in the course of purveying it he provides some clues to what the various libraries held. For example, discussing a particular matter of meaning, he tells that he "made a painstaking search for *A Commentary on Axioms* by Lucius Aelius and I found it in the Library of Peace." Another time, researching a point of grammar, he discovered that "many of the letters of Sinnius Capito . . . have been gathered in one volume, and the volume, I think, is in the Temple of Peace." In both instances he is referring to the library Vespasian built as part of his Temple of Peace; Lucius Aelius was a polymath who was teacher to the greatest of all Roman polymaths, Varro, while Sinnius Capito, a younger contemporary of Varro, wrote on grammar and word-formation. Gellius may have found these books, one perhaps three centuries old and the other perhaps two, in Vespasian's library because it specialized in works of that sort. He mentions that in the library of the Forum of Trajan he came across the edicts of early praetors; possibly it was the repository of historical records of that nature.

The advantage of specialization would have been greater still for the Greek sections. However, even if the libraries did try to practice it, they had imperial whim to contend with. Suetonius reports, for example, that Tiberius was so enamored of the works of Euphorion, Parthenius, and Rhianus that "he enshrined the writings and statues of all of them in the public libraries along with the outstanding authors of the past." They were Greek poets of the Hellenistic period—the first two lived in the third century B.C., the last in the first B.C.—and they were noted and influential. But did all the libraries of Rome need to stock their works? Hadrian and Antoninus Pius once deposited in one of the libraries a copy of a Greek medical treatise in heroic verse that extended to no less than forty books.

For serious study of Greek writings, scholars had to go to Alexandria. For Latin, on the other hand, the best place was Rome. Though the information available enables us to cite but a few random titles that were among the holdings of the Latin chambers in Rome's libraries, we can be certain that everything in the language of value was to be found there. Rome's libraries together did for Latin what Alexandria's single great library did for Greek.

And Rome almost certainly followed Alexandria's practice of making sure that the texts on their shelves were accurate, were as free as possible of scribal errors and other flaws. This was a service of infinite benefit: it directly aided Gellius and his like, lovers of literature who wanted to be certain they were reading the exact words that, say, Vergil had written, and it indirectly aided the buyers of books, for, when they ordered a title from a bookseller that he did not have in stock and sent his scribe to a library to make a copy, they could be sure that what they got had been reproduced from a trustworthy text.

Libraries today acquire most of their books through purchase and some through donations. Rome's public libraries acquired some through donations but most through the making of copies, and a minimum, if any, through purchase.

During Roman Republican times the chief way in which books entered circulation had been through the presentation by authors of copies of their works to friends, fellow writers, patrons, owners of private collections, and the like. It continued to be an important way even after the creation of the public libraries, for authors added these to the list of recipients. They were eager to have their work on the shelves; it was a mark of status as well as entrée to an expanded circle of readers.

Quite likely the libraries acquired most of their holdings of current writings through authors' donations. As for older writings, while donations, such as Tiberius' of the works of three Greek poets of the Hellenistic Age, must have supplied a certain number, the great majority were acquired by arranging to have copies made. The first move of those in charge of stocking the Palatine Library and the Library of the Porticus of Octavia may well have been to send teams of scribes to transcribe books in Pollio's library. Their next might have been to send scribes to homes with extensive private collections. Some of the most noted in Republican times, such as Varro's or Lucullus' or Sulla's, had suffered confiscation because their owners had been on the losing side in Rome's civil wars, but the books presumably were still available in new quarters. Atticus' splendid library certainly was available; by deftly remaining apolitical Atticus had weathered all the political storms and died in his bed in 32 B.C. with his property intact. With Pollio's, Atticus', and other good collections at their disposal, Augustus' people doubtless found right in Rome all the Latin titles they sought and a good many of the Greek. For further Greek titles there was the comprehensive collection at Alexandria to turn to.

We noted earlier that in A.D. 80 the library in the Porticus of Octavia burned down and Domitian restored it. The steps he took to replenish the shelves illustrate the basic ways the imperial libraries made acquisitions. Suetonius reports that he "collected copies from all over and sent people to Alexandria to do transcribing and correcting." To put it less tersely, Domitian ordered copies to be made of whatever titles were available anywhere nearby, no doubt in the other imperial libraries as well as in private collections, and, for what was not, obviously works in Greek, he sent scribes to the library at Alexandria to reproduce texts there. He also had the scribes take with them copies that had been made at Rome whose accuracy was suspect to be checked against the trustworthy versions in Alexandria.

Lastly, the imperial libraries may have now and then purchased titles from Rome's bookstores.

In Republican times the book trade, as we noted, had a poor reputation. Its chief service was supplying books requested by customers, which meant that the dealers had to locate copies to transcribe, and this posed a problem in a city with only private libraries. The arrival of the empire created a new cultural climate that expanded the bookdealers' role. Rome became the center par excellence of Latin learning and literature, and it drew writers, men-of-letters, scholars, students, teachers, and the like, from all over. This climate not only swelled the ranks of bookbuyers but inspired bookstores to provide a new service—having available for ready sale the works of contemporary popular authors, particularly poets.

Our best information about bookstores in the imperial age comes from the satirist Martial, who wrote toward the end of the first century and the beginning of the second. From his remarks it emerges that in his day there were so many of them that they were able to specialize. At least four handled his own works, and three of these stocked different kinds of editions. One bookstore, belonging to a certain Tryphon, sold regular or cheap copies. Martial, for example, says of a fresh publication of his that:

> This little slender book, at Tryphon's store,
> costs just four coppers, and not a penny more.
> Is four too much? It puts you in the red?
> Then pay him two; he'll still come out ahead.

In Atrectus' shop, buyers could find deluxe copies that were highly decorated on the outside and cost much more than ordinary copies. And a third, Secundus', offered a novelty: an edition that was on parchment rather than papyrus and that was not in the form of a roll but of a codex, the ancient equivalent of what we call a book, that is, a gathering of pages written on both sides. This made it particularly convenient for taking along when traveling. As Martial puts it:

> You want to take my poems wherever you go,
> as companions, say, on a trip to some distant land?
> Buy this. It's packed tight into parchment pages, so,
> leave your rolls at home, for this takes just one hand!

It was on sale only at Secundus' shop, so he is careful to give the address:

> Now just in case you don't know the place,
> I'll save you from a wild-goose chase:
> walk past the Temple of Peace, then stop
> and ask for Secundus the freedman's shop.

Authors brought the booksellers their manuscripts and the booksellers had their scribes make multiple copies. The authors got nothing out of the sales; as we pointed out earlier, there was no such thing in the ancient world as copyrights or royalties. It was booksellers like Tryphon and Secundus who pocketed the profits. Martial and his fellow writers willingly cooperated because the stores enabled them to reach many more readers than the circle of friends, patrons, and others to whom they distributed author's copies. And, if they didn't earn any money from the stores, their existence at least saved them some: every copy an author gave out he had to pay to have made up, and it was helpful to be able to suggest to people who importuned him for a copy and to whom he didn't care to give one that they could go to a bookstore. This didn't always work out happily, as we learn from the following dialogue:

> "An author's copy? I've none to spare.
> Try Tryphon's store; you'll find one there."
> "I want you to know there's just no way,
> unless my mind has gone astray,
> that any of your trivia I'd pay money to buy.
> Crazy things I don't do!" "And neither do I."

At least some bookstores stocked weightier works besides currently popular literature. Tryphon, for example, was the publisher—that is, he made up the copies and offered them for sale—of the scholarly Quintilian's comprehensive and lengthy analysis of the training of an orator. At a number of bookstores standard classics, such as Livy's history or Vergil's poems, were available. And there were some that sold old books, antiquarian bookstores in our terminology. Gellius tells how in one in Rome he found "exhibited for sale Fabius' *Annals*, a genuine old copy which the dealer claimed was error-free." The reference is to the magnum opus of the historian Fabius Pictor, who dates from around 200 B.C.

The libraries were unquestionably of great benefit to the bookdealers: when a customer requested a title they did not have on hand, they could, as we have noted, send a scribe to a library and duplicate it. Whether the opposite is true, whether the libraries ever had recourse to the bookstores, is hard to say. Since contemporary writers included the libraries among their recipients of presentation copies, bookstores had nothing to offer on that score. Conceivably items a library might use could turn up at the antiquarian shops. The *bibliothecarii* may have regularly made the rounds of them, just as today's librarians go through used-book catalogues.

Lastly, a word about the services that Rome's libraries offered.

They must have had a scheduled time when they were open to the public, probably from sunrise to about midday, the standard business hours in the Greek and Roman world. The public they served included, besides writers, scholars, lovers of literature and learning, and the like, the scribes these library users sent to do copying for them as well as the scribes bookdealers sent to duplicate titles requested by customers.

Books must have been fetched from the shelves by pages; although we have no proof of this, the alternative, allowing readers to get them themselves, would have been difficult and potentially harmful. The bookcases were numbered, as we noted above, but this provided only a very general clue to a work's location, since each bookcase held several hundred rolls piled on top of each other on the shelves. They were arranged in some way, probably according to the system used in the Greek libraries (see Chap. 3), but even so, finding a given title and extracting it from among its neighbors alongside and on top required someone not only familiar with the holdings but also adept at handling papyrus rolls. A clumsy yank could easily cause damage, since papyrus, although sturdy for writing on, tears easily. For transport from the bookcases, rolls were stacked vertically in buckets of wood or leather; if a request involved a batch of rolls, the bucket was presumably left alongside the reader's chair.

6.8 Stone replica of a leather bucket filled with rolls (part of a statue of Sophocles).

At least some libraries permitted borrowing. Evidence of this privilege emerges clearly from an incident reported by Gellius. He and some friends were staying at a villa near Tibur (Tivoli), and, when they were served melted snow to drink, an expert on Aristotle who happened to be among them warned that, according to Aristotle, this was harmful. To prove his point, he went off to the library in town and came back with the volume of Aristotle's works that contained the passage in question; the library had allowed him to borrow it, even though it must have been a unique copy. From a library at Athens there has survived an inscription which contains the statement that the directors had decided to eliminate borrowing; the implication is that others permitted it. In Rome, Marcus Aurelius and his teacher, as the letter cited previously shows, were able to borrow from either the Palatine Library or Tiberius' library. It has been argued that they were enjoying a special privilege accorded them because of their elevated rank, but this need not necessarily be the case; if borrowing went on outside of Rome, why not in Rome as well?

We have reviewed the public libraries in imperial Rome—what they looked like, how they were staffed, their contents, their methods of acquisition, what services they offered. Let us turn to the rest of the empire.

7

Libraries of the Roman Empire
Outside the City of Rome

In A.D. 395 the vast expanse ruled by Rome, stretching from Britain to the Near East, split into an Eastern and a Western Empire. It was the inevitable result of a fundamental difference. What became the Eastern Empire—Greece, the Greek islands, Asia Minor, the Levant, Egypt—was Greek-speaking and enjoyed a Greek culture that long predated conquest by Rome and that was never displaced, despite the flooding in of Roman soldiers, administrators, traders, businessmen, and others. In what became the Western Empire—Italy, France, Spain, Britain, the northern coast of Africa—the situation was reversed: once the legions had marched in, Latin gradually became the common language and Roman culture prevailed over the various native cultures.

Rome's career of conquest began with Italy, and, by Augustus' time, Latin was established throughout the peninsula as the dominant language and Roman culture the dominant culture. Moreover, by the middle of the first century A.D. literacy had reached a high level, to judge from what we find at Pompeii, that unique supplier of information about Roman daily life. On the walls of rooms and the façades of houses and other surfaces, there are hundreds of graffiti; they were so well protected over the centuries by the blanket of volcanic ash that covered the town, they can still be read. The most rudimentary arc, in their way, the most revealing—letters of the alphabet scrawled low down on the walls of rooms, undoubtedly the work of youngsters practicing their ABCs. And it must have been children further along in their education who, echoing what they were learning at school, produced the graffiti that consist of scraps of lines from Vergil (*arma virumque cano*— "I sing of arms and the man," the opening words of the *Aeneid*— is common). Many Pompeians wrote on the walls about their amorous joys or sorrows; some were not merely literate but literary, able to express their feelings by quoting verses from Propertius, Tibullus, and Ovid, Rome's love poets par excellence. The artists who decorated the walls bear witness to Pompeii's literacy no less than the scribblers who defaced them: they painted scenes that include figures reading rolls, they drew portraits showing men holding rolls and women holding notes, they included among the subjects of their still lifes writing instruments and materials—pen, ink, rolls, tablets. Clearly, reading and writing were not limited to an elite upper crust of the town's population. And there is no reason to think that Pompeii was exceptional; other Italian communities must have been equally literate.

So it is no surprise that there were public libraries at Pompeii and elsewhere in Italy. At Pompeii the actual remains have been uncovered; elsewhere they are attested by inscriptions—which incidentally inform us that, like the public libraries of Hellenistic times (Chap. 4) or for that matter our own Carnegie libraries, the money for them came not from government funds but from generous donors. An inscription from Comum (Como) records that the younger Pliny, who was a native son, among other gifts gave his

7.1 Lover's graffito, in fluent Latin cursive writing, found on a wall in Pompeii. It is in the form of an elegiac couplet: *Quis[quis] amat valeat, pereat qui nescit amare./ Bis tanto pereat quisquis amare vetat.* "Long life to whoever is in love and death to whoever is ignorant of love. Death twice over to whoever forbids being in love."

birthplace a library along with a fund of 100,000 sesterces (equivalent perhaps to some $400,000 in purchasing power) to maintain it. An inscription from Suessa Aurunca (near the coast, about two-thirds of the way from Rome to Naples) mentions a *bibliotheca Matidiana*; the name makes it almost certain that it was a *bibliotheca* that had been donated by Matidia, mother-in-law of Hadrian. At Volsinii (Bolsena, near Orvieto) an inscription reports that a townsman provided a library and the books for it. Tibur had a library, as we know from the anecdote in Gellius discussed at the end of the previous chapter. These are the few whose existence has by chance entered the historical record; there surely were others that have disappeared without trace.

Eastward of Italy, in the Greek-speaking part of the empire libraries, as we have seen, had been in existence since Hellenistic times. In the first and second centuries A.D., when, along with the rest of the Mediterranean world, it enjoyed the peace and prosperity of the *Pax Romana*, still more libraries were built at a number of major centers. These reveal the impact of the new rulers: they are almost all of the Roman type, reading rooms with the books shelved along the walls.

Alexandria had fallen into Roman hands along with the rest of Egypt in 30 B.C. Its great library was kept up and, during the reign of Claudius, was expanded by a "Claudian Addition" where once every year one of the two histories this scholarly emperor had authored—a history of the Etruscans, running to twenty books, and a history of Carthage, running to eight—was read aloud from beginning to end; the other was read somewhere in the original building. Because the learned Claudius had written them in Greek, not Latin, the language posed no problem for Alexandrian listeners. It is a reasonable assumption that the new addition, besides serving as an audience chamber, housed copies of the histories so that they could be available for consultation at all times and not just for hearing on a single annual occasion. The architects could easily have taken care of this by adding to the specifications a few Roman-style bookcase-niches in the walls—or perhaps more than a few, to accommodate selected works in Greek by other Roman authors as well. (Whether Alexandria's holdings ever included any in Latin is an open question.)

Alexandria's rival, the library at Pergamum, had come under the control of the Romans a century earlier, shortly after 133 B.C., when they took over the kingdom of the Attalids. They obviously kept that library going right up to the time of Mark Antony's dalliance with Cleopatra, that is, the years leading up to the battle of Actium in 31 B.C., because, as we noted earlier (Chap. 3), one of his exaggerated gestures of affection was to make a gift to her of the 200,000 volumes in it (she presumably added them to the Alexandrian collection). We are told this by a not very trustworthy informant, but there could be truth in his words. The Attalids had created the library to enhance the cultural image of their regime; now that they were gone, so was its reason for being—and so were the royal funds that covered the cost of maintaining it. Antony's act may have been a shrewd way of getting rid of something that might have become a financial burden and for which, from his point of view, there was no particular need.

In the reign of Hadrian, Pergamum acquired another library, much smaller in size than the Attalids' and very different in purpose. On the outskirts of the city was a sanctuary of Asclepius, which grew into a celebrated health center. Here, besides buildings for treatment of the patients, were amenities to help them pass the time, such as porticoes for leisurely walks and a theater for various kinds of performances. A surviving inscription records that a generous local woman, Flavia Melitine, added a library. Its remains have been discovered, and they show that it was typically Roman, a room with niches for bookcases and, at the center of the back wall, an apse for a statue. It was of good size, 16.52 m along the front and back and 18.50 m along the sides, but low, with only one level of niches, whose total number came to sixteen—two on each side of the apse and six in each of the side walls. Melitine's gift was, in effect, an ample reading room with a modest collection, just what casual readers, such as those at the health center presumably were, would find most useful.

Athens under the Roman Empire was still culturally important,

and in the early decades of the second century it gained two new libraries. One was conveniently located at the southeast corner of
the agora, where excavators uncovered the inscription that was on
it. This stated that "Titus Flavius Pantainos . . . dedicated to Trajan
. . . and the city of Athens out of his own pocket the colonnades,
the area surrounded by them, the library with its books, and all the
decoration involved." Only scant remains of the structure itself
have survived; they seem to show that Pantainos had his library
built in the traditional Greek fashion, a series of small rooms
fronting on a portico.

Some two hundred meters to the northeast of Pantainos' was
another library, a handsome gift to the city from the emperor
Hadrian. It was actually a combination of library and cloister, a
spreading rectangular complex that measured all of 82 m along the
sides and 60 m along the front and back. A wall enclosed the
whole, with the colonnade of the cloister running inside it. Along
the sides the wall bulged outward at three points to create recesses
where people could sit at their leisure, while the large open area in
the middle was given over to a garden and pool. The rear wall was
set back from the colonnade to make space for a line of chambers,
the central one of which was bigger than the others, about 23 m
along the front and rear and 13 m along the sides. This was the library, and, as we might expect of a donation from a Roman emperor, was of Roman style, the walls lined with niches. Its front
wall lay parallel to the colonnade of the cloister and, like the libraries in the bathing establishments at Rome, had as entrance an
opening on to the colonnade. The opening had no doors but
merely four columns standing at equal intervals; very likely the intervals were spanned by bronze gates hung on the columns to per-
mit the closing of the library during off-hours. The back wall of the
chamber had the customary apse for a statue. The niches were of
usual size, 2.80 m high and 1.20 m wide and .50 m deep, and,
though only remains of one level survive, the indications are that
there were two more above it. This setup allowed for a good many
niches: it has been reckoned that there were sixty-six in all, almost
double the number in each of the chambers of Trajan's library at

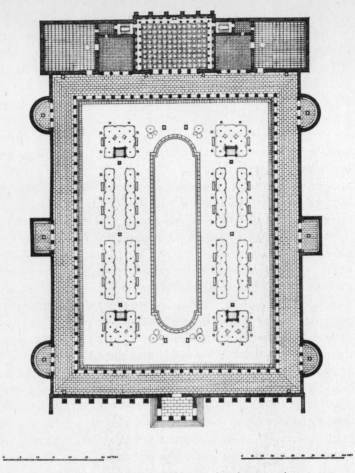

7.2 Plan of the cloister and library of Hadrian at Athens.

Rome (see Chap. 6). The niches there, however, were much wider and very likely higher.

Around the same time as Athens received its sumptuous gift from Hadrian, Ephesus, seat of the Roman governor of the province in which it was located and the major seaport on the western coast of Asia Minor, was given a library that was smaller but equally sumptuous. It was erected, a number of inscriptions inform us, by

7.3 Reconstruction of the west end of the complex of cloister and library built by Hadrian at Athens. The taller building in the center is the library.

Tiberius Julius Aquila Polemaeanus as both a donation to his city and a memorial to his father, who had been a man of even greater distinction than the son. Aquila, we learn from one of the inscriptions, died before completion of the structure, which probably was around A.D. 135:

> For Tiberius Julius Celsus Polemaeanus, consul, proconsul of Asia [i.e., governor of the province], Tiberius Julius Aquila Polemaeanus, consul, his son, set up the Library of Celsus with his own money, along with its decoration, statuary, and books. He left for its maintenance and for the purchase of books 25,000 denarii [the equivalent in purchasing power of perhaps $400,000]. . . . The heirs of Aquila have completed it.

So extensive are the remains that the archaeologists have been able to reconstruct the building almost in its entirety. The results are dramatic: visitors today see a nearly intact Roman library that is at the same time an architectural showpiece. The most remarkable

7.4 Façade of the library of Celsus at Ephesus. Circa A.D. 135.

feature is the façade, all of marble and in two levels elaborately adorned with columns, prominent aedicula, and a number of statues. A flight of eight steps spanning the width leads up to the lower level, which has three handsome doorways flanked by aedicula that shelter female statues. As inscriptions on the bases tell, these represent Wisdom, Virtue, and Knowledge—qualities exemplified by Celsus and, at the same time, goals that one can seek through the resources of a library. The second level has three aedicula, topped by massive pediments, that frame large windows. The interior is a lofty rectangular chamber, 16.70 m along the front and back and 10.90 m along the sides, fitted out in standard Roman fashion with an apse for a statue and niches for bookcases. The niches measured 2.80 m high and 1 m wide and .50 m deep, rather narrower than usual, and there were three levels of them. In the back wall the apse, rising almost to the roof, was flanked on each side at each level by two niches, while the side walls had each three levels of three; there were thus thirty niches in all, capable of holding, at a very rough estimate, some 3,000 rolls. Under the niches of the bottom level ran a podium 1 m high and 1.20 m deep; on it

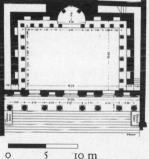

0   5   10 m

7.5 Reconstruction and plan of the interior of the library of Celsus at
   Ephesus.

rested the columns that held up the gallery providing access to the
niches of the second level, and this in turn held up the columns
supporting the gallery of the third level. The roof was flat and may
have had an oculus, a round opening in the center, to add light.
Clearly more attention was paid to the beauty and impressiveness
of the structure than to the size of the collection in it. This is under-
standable: the remains of the man in whose memory it was built

rested in a monumental sarcophagus in an underground chamber beneath the apse The building was a mausoleum as well as library.

When we turn to the western half of the Roman Empire, a curious picture emerges. Throughout what is today England, Spain, France, and the northern coast of Africa, we have proof of the existence of libraries in but two places, Carthage in Tunisia and Timgad in Algeria.

We know there was a library at Carthage because a Roman writer of the second century A.D. happens to mention it. The original Carthage, the great Punic capital, had been razed to the ground by the Romans in 146 B.C. Augustus built up a new city on the site, and it grew to be next to Rome in size and importance, achieving particular fame as an educational center. That it had a library is what we would expect.

Timgad—or Thamugadi, to use its ancient name—was founded by Trajan in A.D. 100 and quickly became a flourishing town. We know it had a library only because of the unusually comprehensive archaeological investigation that the site received. Excavators laid the whole ancient town bare and on one of the main streets they uncovered the remains of a building identified by an inscription as a library. It had been paid for, as so often elsewhere, by a generous citizen. There are no indications of date, but certain clues point to the third century, perhaps even later; thus at least a century and very likely more had passed before the town got a library. The building was unusual, being apsidal in shape and roofed by a semi-dome—a sort of free-standing, small-sized version of the library area in the baths of Trajan at Rome (see Chap. 6). In the center of the curving wall of the apse was a space for a statue, and on either side were four niches for bookcases, 1.25 m wide and .50 m deep and doubtless some 2 m or more high; the upper portions are lost, so we cannot be sure. A small narrow room flanked the apsidal chamber on either side; these almost certainly were for storage of books, since the eight niches of the library proper could not have accommodated much of a collection, even one limited, as was no doubt the case here, to Latin titles alone.

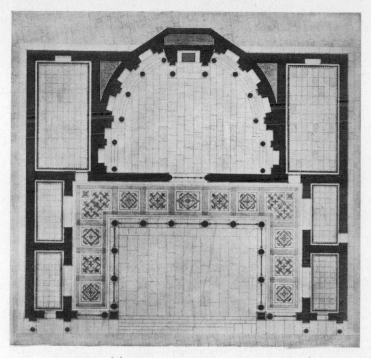

7.6 Plan of the library at Timgad. Third century A.D.

Thamugadi boasts the distinction of having the sole library attested either archaeologically or in inscriptions in the vast span of the Roman Empire west of Italy. This was certainly not because the town was culturally unique, a lone oasis in a backward wasteland. Roman domination had thoroughly urbanized and Romanized the whole of the west, had replaced native settlements with a network of communities, great and small, in which the language of everyday life was Latin and the culture Roman. By imperial times, literacy, if not as deepseated and pervasive as in the Greek-speaking portion of the empire, was widespread. There were schoolmasters teaching elementary classes in Latin in all major towns, while the cities offered more advanced classes and in certain great cities, such as Carthage or Marseilles, one might get the equivalent of univer-

7.7 Cast of the remains of the library at Timgad.

sity training. Martial, for example, was born in Bilbilis, a city in northeastern Spain, and did not leave there for Rome until he was in his early twenties; it was at Bilbilis that he got the education underlying his astonishing skill in handling the Latin language. Bilbilis, it would seem, was as likely a locale for a library as Carthage, and so were a dozen other important centers. And there must have been a multitude of towns beside Timgad whose population included men and women with the wealth and cultural ambition to bestow a library upon their fellow denizens.

That only two libraries are attested in the Roman west is almost certainly not because there were that few but rather because whatever others there were have slipped through the cracks of the historical record. Our information about the existence of ancient libraries, as about so many aspects of the ancient world, derives from haphazard sources. We know of a library at Carthage only because of a writer's casual remark; we know of one at Timgad only because of the exceptionally thorough excavation of the site. It so happens that, in the miscellany of Greek and Roman writings that through hit-or-miss circumstance have come down to us, no mention occurs of libraries at, say, Marseilles or Narbonne, although there is every reason to think they existed there. And when archaeologists dig other sites as comprehensively as Timgad, they may well find an inscription recording a benefactor's gift of a library or unearth the remains of a building with the characteristic bookcase-niches in its walls.

When we turn to the question of what the provincial libraries had on their shelves, the information is equally haphazard.

It is a reasonable assumption that the heart of their collections consisted of standard authors. There is some confirmation of this in an inscription from Halicarnassus, the city on the southwestern coast of Asia Minor that enjoyed the renown of having been the birthplace of Herodotus. It records the official honors heaped on a local luminary, a writer of tragedy named Gaius Julius Longianus. These included the putting of his books "in our libraries so that our young people may learn from them in the same way they learn from the writings of the ancients." The clear implication is that the youth of Halicarnassus had available in the libraries (apparently there was more than one) the works of the writers of long ago, of Homer, Euripides, certainly the city's cherished Herodotus, and so on; to this time-honored company Longianus' writings were to be added.

That town libraries included in their holdings the publications of local authors may well have been a common practice; it is attested at Rhodiapolis, an inland town of southwestern Asia Minor, as well as at Halicarnassus. The author in this instance was a physician who, in addition to practicing medicine, wrote treatises on the subject. These were in verse, as was not uncommon, and they gained him such fame that among certain learned intellectual groups he was known as the "Homer of medical poetry." The ruling bodies at Rhodiapolis authorized the erection of an inscription in honor of this doctor-poet of theirs, and among the numerous manifestations of his good will recorded on it was his donating of copies of his works to his hometown.

The collections at Halicarnassus, Rhodiapolis, and elsewhere in the east consisted almost exclusively of books in Greek. The archaeological remains of Hadrian's library at Athens, Celsus' at Ephesus, and others conformably show only one chamber. There are no examples of the twin chambers of the libraries at Rome where the holdings were in both Latin and Greek. In the libraries of the west the books presumably were almost exclusively in Latin, hence the single chamber at Timgad.

But there were exceptions—exceptions that reveal the presence of some unexpected titles on the shelves of local libraries. We learn about them from the experiences of that indefatigable user of libraries, Aulus Gellius (see Chap. 6). In the library at Tibur (Tivoli) he was able to consult the *Annals* of Claudius Quadrigarius, a Roman historian of the early decades of the first century B.C. It was in Latin, to be sure, but it was hardly a standard work. The great surprise at Tibur emerges from Gellius' account of a scholarly wrangle among some literati staying at a nearby villa about a statement in Aristotle (see Chap. 6 ad fin.). The disputants were able to settle it because Tibur's library had a set of Aristotle's writings, a holding that presumably would be found only in the very biggest libraries.

Then there was the astonishing discovery Gellius made at Patras, the flourishing city on the northwestern coast of the Peloponnese. In the library there he came across "a copy, of unquestionable antiquity" (*librum verae vetustatis*) of Livius Andronicus' translation into Latin of the *Odyssey* (see Chap. 5 in init.). The title it bore, he notes, was not the Latin title but the Greek, written in Greek letters. This could very well have been for the convenience of the pages and other library personnel who were unfamiliar with the Roman alphabet; our libraries transliterate Arabic or Hebrew titles into English letters for similar reasons. What was a translation into archaic Latin of Homer's epic doing in the library of a city where the population was Greek and the original could be purchased at any bookshop? Augustus had settled a considerable number of Roman soldiers at Patras and there doubtless were other Roman residents, but any among them with the education to make use of Patras' library would have been able to read the poem in the original. Gellius emphasizes that the copy he saw was genuinely old, and this makes it sound like a rare book, something a bibliophile would have owned. Could some local bibliophile have acquired it during a trip to Italy and brought it home, and on his death his heirs donated it to the library?

In sum, provincial libraries contained chiefly the standard classics, but also the writings of local notables in places that boasted such, and, here and there, an unusual work that somehow had made its way onto the shelves.

8

From Roll to Codex

Until the second century A.D. library holdings were all in the form of rolls, some of parchment but the majority of papyrus. When the curtain goes up on the early Middle Ages half a millennium or so later, codices, in shape and make-up like the modern book, have replaced the roll, and they are chiefly of parchment. The roll continued to serve for documents and the like, writings of the sort that go into files or archives, but the codex took over in literature, scientific studies, technical manuals, and so on, writings of the sort that go onto library shelves. It was a change that profoundly affected all who dealt with books, from casual readers to professional librarians.

The earliest references to codices occur in Martial, not only in the poem we discussed previously (Chap. 6), which was published in A.D. 85/86, but in a collection of couplets that appeared a year or so before. Each couplet was to accompany a gift. One, bearing the title "Ovid's *Metamorphoses* on *Membranae*," runs as follows:

> This bulky mass of multiple folds
> all fifteen poems of Ovid holds.

The word *membranae*, literally "skins," is the name the Romans gave to a codex of parchment; the gift the couplet went with must have been a copy that contained the work in its entirety, all fifteen books, and that was in the form of a codex and not, as was usual at the time, of a roll. Other couplets reveal that among the gifts were codex copies of Vergil, Cicero, and Livy. Martial's words give the distinct impression that such editions were something recently introduced.

The codex was the offspring of the wooden writing tablet that the ancients for centuries had used for jotting down notes (see Chap. 2). When more space was needed than was offered by the surface of a single board, they stacked a number of them and bound them together by drilling holes along one edge and passing a cord through the holes, creating in this way a notebook; examples have been found with as many as ten boards. In the course of time deluxe models made with tablets of ivory instead of wood became available. The Roman name for the tablet notebook was *codex;* only much later did the term acquire the sense we give to it. At some point the Romans devised a lighter and less clumsy notebook by substituting parchment sheets for the wood or ivory tablets: they laid two or more sheets on top of each other, folded them down the middle, pierced holes along the crease, and passed a cord through to hold them together. It was but a short step from binding up a few parchment sheets for the jotting down of notes to binding up a quantity of them for the inscribing of extended texts—to creating, in other words, a codex in the later sense of the term.

To the Romans goes the credit for this vital step. They must have taken it some decades before the end of the first century A.D., for by then, as we can tell from Martial's couplets, editions of standard authors in codex form were available at Rome, although still a novelty. Because Rome was the center of the book trade in Latin works, it's safe to conclude that the production of such editions originated there. The great advantage they offered over rolls was capacity, an advantage arising from the fact that the outside face of a roll was left blank, whereas both sides of each leaf of a codex had writing on it, as in a modern book. "How small a tablet contains immense Vergil!" Martial marvels in one of his couplets; the *Aeneid* alone would have required four or more rolls.

The codices he was familiar with were of parchment; in the lines to accompany a gift of a copy of Homer, for example, he describes it as being of "leather in many folds." But they were also made up of sheets of papyrus. In Egypt, the home of the papyrus plant and the center for manufacturing it into writing material, the papyrus

8.1 Portrait of a Pompeian couple. They emphasize their literacy: he holds a roll, she a wooden tablet in her left hand and a stylus for writing on it in her right.

codex was, not surprisingly, more common than the parchment: among the thousands of pieces of Greek and Latin writing that the dry sands there have preserved (see Chap. 4), about 550 are from codices, and slightly more than 70 percent of these are of papyrus. Presumably the papyrus codex was the more common outside of Egypt as well. When the Greeks and Romans had only the roll for writing books, they preferred papyrus to parchment (see Chap. 2). There is every reason to think they applied the same preference to the codex when it became available.

The finds from Egypt enable us to trace the gradual replacement

9.2 Wooden writing tablet, 21.5 cm × 13.5 cm, with ten leaves. Seventh century A.D.

of the roll by the codex. It made its appearance there not long after Martial's day, in the second century A.D., at the very earliest toward the end of the first. Its debut was modest. Over 1,330 pieces of Greek literary, scientific, and other such writings have been discovered that date to the first and second centuries; all are on rolls save less than twenty, a mere 1.5 percent, on codices. In the third century the percentage rises from 1.5 percent to about 17 percent; clearly the codex was gaining favor. Around A.D. 300 the percentage has climbed to 50 percent—a parity with the roll that is reflected in some preserved representations, which picture a man holding a roll next to one holding a codex. By A.D. 400 it is up to 80 percent and by A.D. 500 to 90 percent. The roll still had centuries of

8.3 Drawing of a tomb painting, fifth century A.D., showing the deceased (in nobleman's dress) holding a codex and, to the right of him, St. Peter holding a roll.

life ahead of it, but only for documents; what people read for pleasure, edification, or instruction was virtually all on codices.

Egypt furnishes information not only on the growing use of codices but also on their composition. Though most of the specimens found are in fragmentary condition, frequently just a page or part of a page, in a few cases enough pages survive to reveal how they were put together. Within these cases, few as they are, there is a good deal of variation; probably the book-makers were experimenting as they felt their way in the handling of the new format. Some codices were made like an oversize notebook, merely a pile of sheets folded down the middle with a cord through holes in the crease to keep them together. When this primitive type was used for a long text requiring many sheets, the result was bulky and liable to split or tear along the spine. Usually codices were made up of quires sewn together, just as books are today. The quires may be of single sheets, each folded down the center, but far more often they are of a number of sheets, from two to as many as eight. And a mix of quires can occur: in one extreme example, the sequence of quires runs: 5-sheet, 4-sheet, 1-sheet, 5-sheet, 5-sheet, 8-sheet.

Eventually the 4-sheet quire, which produces 8 leaves and 16 pages, became the norm, so much so that its Latin name, *quaternio* "foursome" is the etymological ancestor of the word "quire."

It took a long time, from about A.D. 100 to after 400, for the codex to supplant the roll. Yet its advantages were obvious from the outset. When it was newly on the market, Martial, as we pointed out, recognized one advantage, its greater capacity, a feature that made it particularly convenient for travelers. Another was ease of access to the contents: a reader of a roll who was looking for a particular passage had to keep rolling up with one hand and unrolling with the other, whereas readers of codices merely flipped pages. Moreover, after finding what they sought, if they wanted to refer to it again, they could keep a finger on the page or slide in a piece of papyrus to flag it while they went on reading. For a codex, like a modern book, could be held in one hand, leaving the other free to mark a place, take notes, reach for another codex, even chase away an annoying fly or scratch an itch. A further advantage of the codex was that it was customarily bound between covers, most often of wood, and this kept the pages safe from damage; rolls were piled up on the shelves, or stacked in boxes or buckets, with no protection. And codices might have their titles inscribed along an edge or elsewhere and so were always identifiable; a roll had its title on a label that was attached to one end and could come loose and fall off.

Why, then, did the adoption of the codex take so long? A key reason surely was the heavy weight of habit. Readers were accustomed to rolls; the codex was new and strange, it took getting used to. The same was true for the scriptoria's craftsmen: for centuries the book-makers had been putting together rolls, and the copyists writing on them.

There is, however, one striking exception to the laggard transition from roll to codex. The finds from Egypt demonstrate unequivocally that from the very beginning Christians used only the codex for their copies of the Bible and strongly favored it for their other religious writings. The earliest preserved copies of the Bible date to the second century or the beginning of the third; there are eleven that belong to this period (six containing parts of the Septuagint, the Greek translation of the Old Testament that is traditionally dated about 270 B.C., and five containing parts of the New) and every one of these eleven is a codex. This is in striking contrast to the examples of pagan literary, scientific, and other such works from the same period: out of a total of more than 1,200, a mere thirty are codices, less than 3 percent. If we move further down in time to include Bibles dating up to the beginning of the fifth century, the figure rises from eleven to around 170; among them are a few on rolls, fourteen to be precise—but thirteen of the fourteen can be explained by special factors, leaving a sole exceptional instance of a roll bearing Christian Scripture.

This favoring of the codex by the Christians may well have originated where the codex itself seems to have, in Rome. By the second half of the first century A.D., the time when the Gospels were being put down in writing, an important Christian community had been built up in the city. This was also when, as Martial's poems show, the codex form of book made its appearance there. The local clergy, for whom the Scriptures served almost as a handbook, may have chosen it for its obvious greater convenience over the roll for such a purpose. And it undoubtedly had the advantage of being free of the associations the roll had—the roll of parchment with Jewish writings, the roll of papyrus with pagan. In any event, wherever the choice was originally made, whether at Rome or elsewhere, as Christianity expanded, so did its use of the codex, and when, from Constantine's reign on, Christianity was more or less the established religion, codices were to be seen in every church and school of the empire. This surely speeded up the overall displacement of the roll.

We have been able to follow the shift from roll to codex through the finds from Egypt. The same finds throw the only light we have on the fortunes of the papyrus codex vis-à-vis the parchment. Theoretically, in Egypt, the one land blessed with local supplies of papyrus, the codex of papyrus should have reigned supreme. That is not the case: the codex of parchment makes its appearance there at the same time as the codex of papyrus, the second century A.D. Although the eleven codices of the Bible dating to that century that we discussed happen to be of papyrus, there are some eighteen codices of the same century with pagan writings, and of these four are of parchment. Moreover, an illuminating bit of information turns up in a more or less contemporary letter that was recovered from an Egyptian village; in it a son tells his father that:

> Deios came to us and showed us the six parchment codices. We
> didn't choose any but we collated eight others for which I gave
> 100 drachmas on account.

Deios, apparently an itinerant bookseller, was peddling a stock of no less than fourteen parchment codices, and these were of interest to a resident of an Egyptian village. The parchment codex had traveled far and briskly from Martial's Rome.

In the third century, when the use of codices became widespread, the parchment codex held its own. The total number of surviving codices that date to this century is more than one hundred; at least seventeen of these are parchment, around 16 percent. In the fourth century the percentage rises to about 35 percent—of some 160 codices, some 50 are parchment—and remains roughly at that level in the fifth. In short, even in Egypt, the ancient world's source of papyrus, the parchment codex commanded a significant share of the market.

No such statistics are available for the Greco-Roman world outside of Egypt, because too few codices from the relevant centuries have survived there. We get some help, however, from remarks in several fourth-century writers; these indicate that there the codex of papyrus was steadily giving way to the codex of parchment. Jerome, in a letter of about 385, mentions the library that Pamphilus had put together for the church at Caesarea, where he had been priest at the end of the third century and beginning of the fourth, and adds that the library "was partially ruined, and Acacius and Euzoius, priests of that church, undertook to renew it in parchment"—in other words, transferred texts from codices of papyrus that had suffered severe damage over the years to codices of parchment, which would be more durable. The emperor Constantine around 325 informs the ecclesiastical scholar Eusebius that he is issuing orders that there be written for use by the clergy "fifty copies, portable and easy to read, on well-prepared parchment, . . . of the Divine Scriptures." His choice of codices of parchment over papyrus was doubtless determined not only by their greater ability to withstand wear—wear that in this instance included being carried about—but also by the fact that, when made of parchment of high quality, which was the case here, they could be assembled with enough pages to hold the entire Bible. The largest surviving papyrus codex of the Bible, for example, does not contain even the entire New Testament, just the Gospels and Acts. The famous Codex Sinaiticus, written on fine parchment, contained the Old Testament, the New Testament, and some apocryphal books to boot. A letter of St. Basil dating 374–375 reveals that, for editions of quality, parchment was mandatory. It is addressed to Amphilochius, Bishop of Iconium, and in it he explains to Amphilochius that he was planning to send a copy of his *On the Holy Spirit* but "the brethren who are with me prevented me from sending it written on papyrus, saying that they had orders from you to write it on parchment."

These comments come from Christian writers, but the status parchment had attained was not limited to their circles. A Latin poet of about 400, in a set of verses he composed to accompany a presentation copy of his works, proudly proclaims that his "poems are worthy of parchment pages" and apologizes for the fact that, because he lives out in the countryside where writing materials are hard to come by, he must send them "inscribed on the reedy fabric of the Nilotic papyrus."

The oldest codices to have survived from outside of Egypt are no earlier than the fourth and fifth centuries and in number but a handful—several of the Bible, several of Vergil, one of Homer, a few others. All are of parchment. All, as it happens, are elegant editions, written in calligraphic hands on very thin leaves of parchment. For deluxe copies such as these, papyrus, it would seem, was out of the question.

In at least one area, Roman law, the parchment codex served for cheap editions as well as fine. The titles of the celebrated compilations, the Codex Theodosianus, promulgated in 438, and the Codex Justinianus, promulgated in 529, indicate that the emperors had them inscribed on codices, unquestionably of parchment since it offered both greater durability and greater capacity, and unquestionably of parchment of high quality since the books were being done under imperial auspices. At the other end of the scale, remarks dropped by Libanius, a fourth-century intellectual whose multifarious activities included teaching law, show that his students' textbooks were also parchment codices. There were good reasons for this: parchment could take the hard treatment such books got, and the codex format permitted the quick and easy checking of the wording of statutes, judicial decisions, and so on. The parchment that went into them must have been the lowest grade, skins so thick that the books ended up heavy enough to make a student lugging them sag at the knees. The weight also provided an extracurricular virtue: in student fights, the books could be used instead of rocks for heaving at opponents.

Pliny the Younger tells in one of his letters how his uncle, Pliny the Elder, author of a massive encyclopedia as well as several other lengthy works, was able to write so much and still carry on a career as a full-time Roman official: he exploited every off-duty moment. A typical example was his attitude toward walking: one doesn't walk, one takes litters because that way one can utilize the time en route for study. His method of conducting research, his nephew explains, was "to have a book read aloud while he made notes and extracts." Pliny lived in the first century A.D., when books were in the form of rolls; by employing a reader he saved the time it would have taken, whenever he came upon something that called for a note, to put down the roll he was working with, pick up tablets and stylus, and, after jotting his note, put these down and pick up the roll again. When, three centuries later, Jerome was making his translation of the Bible into Latin, he had a codex open to the passage he was dealing with and a hand free to write his rendition The replacement of roll by codex, in a word, had a profound effect

8.4 Detail of a mosaic in the Mausoleum of Gallia Placidia at Ravenna, fifth century A.D., showing a bookcase with doors open and codices of the Gospels lying on the shelves.

upon the ease and speed of research, comparable perhaps to that of the introduction of the xerox copier in our own day.

The codex had an equally profound effect upon the operations of libraries. Before the arrival of the codex, library shelves were filled with papyrus rolls piled one on top of the other. Extracting a given roll or batch of rolls involved moving those surrounding it, a procedure that had to be done with care to avoid inflicting damage. Codices, on the other hand, were kept flat on the shelf in neat stacks, their leaves protected by covers; any desired title could be easily and swiftly extracted. When a reader in Pliny's day requested, say, the works of Vergil, the page had to pull out a batch of rolls and load them into a leather bucket to carry them over, and the reader had to rummage through the bucketful to find the particular roll he wanted to start with; in Jerome's day the page would have pulled out and brought over a single codex. When it came to the consulting of library catalogues, the coming of the codex must have effected a veritable transformation. Before then a catalogue consisted of a collection of rolls; looking up a title involved finding the roll which contained the appropriate category, unrolling that roll until one reached the category, and then slowly continuing to unroll until the title turned up. Once catalogues were in codex form, users merely flipped pages to find category and title.

Trajan's library at Rome, Hadrian's at Athens, Celsus' at Ephesus, all the public libraries throughout the empire, in the last centuries of their existence had to work out ways of integrating new acquisitions in codex form with the rolls on their shelves. The libraries that next came into existence had no such problem: they served institutions whose reading matter had been in codex form from the outset—Christian churches, schools, monasteries. Let us turn to these libraries.

9

Toward the Middle Ages

By the beginning of the fifth century A.D. the Roman Empire had undergone two fundamental changes, one political and the other spiritual. It had split into halves, each ruled by its own emperor, a western with its capital at Ravenna or Milan and an eastern with its capital at Constantinople. In both, Christianity had emerged as the prevailing religion.

The rise and triumph of Christianity had a profound effect upon literature: it elevated religion into a predominant concern. To be sure, there were still writers, in both Greek and Latin, who dealt with secular subjects, but they are minor compared with the great Christian authors, the likes of Basil or Eusebius in Greek, of Augustine or Jerome in Latin. There was an outpouring of studies of the text of the Bible, commentaries on passages and interpretations of them, discussions of the nature of the divine, diatribes against views held to be heretical, and so on. Such literature was out of place on the shelves of the libraries that existed; it required its own libraries. These arose as part of Christian churches, monasteries, and the like and, spreading far and wide during the Middle Ages, were steps in the progression toward the libraries of today.

Of the two halves of the empire, the eastern, the Byzantine Empire as it came to be called, fared much better than the western.

The western empire did not hold together very long. In the fifth and sixth centuries invasions of Goths, Vandals, and others succeeded in putting Spain and Gaul and large parts of Italy under the rule of barbarian kings. Italy had been the home of town libraries up and down the peninsula in the prosperous days of the Roman Empire; these disappeared as town upon town fell under the rule of Ostrogoths in the sixth century. And, after Justinian, the powerful head of the eastern empire from 527 to 565, elected to drive the invaders out and the armies he sent struggled for two decades to do it, much of central Italy became the scene of destructive warfare, with Rome itself suffering both siege and sack. In the days of Augustus and Trajan, when the city was home to splendid public libraries, it had had a population of over a million; during these bloody years the number dropped to a low of 30,000. Shrunken and ravaged, it had neither the funds to support libraries nor the people to use them.

The eastern empire, spared barbarian invasions, lived much more tranquilly and lasted much longer, up until 1453, when the Turks completed their conquest of it with the capture of Constantinople. Constantinople had been founded by Constantine the Great in 324; in 330 he chose it to be the imperial capital instead of Rome, and after the empire split it remained capital of the eastern half. Here was the emperor's palace and here also was the residence of one of the four patriarchs who headed the Christian world of the east (the others were at Antioch, Jerusalem, and Alexandria). Constantinople gradually added cultural luster to its political stature. In 425 the emperor Theodosius II established thirty-one professorial chairs, mostly in Greek and Latin rhetoric and language plus several in law, thereby creating the equivalent of a university. Then, during the reign of Justinian, the erection of St. Sophia gave the city an architectural work of foremost quality, while the compilation of the Codex Justinianus, the magisterial summary of Roman law commissioned by the emperor, gave it distinction as a center of legal study. It boasted three major libraries. Two were basically secular, one at the university for the faculty and students, and the other at the palace for the royal family and the civil service. The university library seems to have remained in existence into the Middle Ages, the palace library right up to the taking over of the city by the Turks in 1453. The third was a theological collection at the seat of the patriarchy.

These three ended up as the ranking libraries of the eastern empire, because possible rivals elsewhere within its borders gradually ceased to be, especially after the Arab conquests in the Near East between 636 and 642 put Syria and Palestine and Egypt under Muslim rule. The celebrated library at the Museum at Alexandria was already gone by about 270, as we mentioned in an earlier chapter (Chap. 3 ad fin.). The second most important Alexandrian library was at the temple of the god Serapis, the Serapeum, and in 390 this building was razed when Theophilus, patriarch of Alexandria at the time and a man of violent temper, zealously carried out the decree of Emperor Theodosius II to close all pagan places of worship. The library, however, may have escaped destruction and still been in existence when Alexandria capitulated to the Arabs in 642, if we can believe a picturesque tale preserved in Arab sources. This relates that a Greek savant, who was a friend of the commander of the army that took over the city, asked him for the library as a gift. The commander prudently referred the matter to his overlord, Caliph Omar, and was told: "If these writings of the Greeks agree with the book of God, they are useless and need not be preserved; if they disagree, they are pernicious and ought to be destroyed." And destroyed they were, by being handed over to the city's baths for fuel, and, the story specifies, they sufficed to feed the furnaces of all four thousand of them for six months.

After 642 the patriarchy's library at Constantinople very likely was the eastern empire's best theological collection, since the cities where the other notable collections were located—the cities where Christianity had arisen and the early Church Fathers had lived and worked and gathered the writings they needed to carry on their studies—were now under the domination of the Arabs, who presumably applied Caliph Omar's reasoning to whatever libraries they came across. Ever since the first half of the third century, there had been a collection at Jerusalem, apparently housed in the Church of the Holy Sepulchre. Alexander, Jerusalem's bishop at the time, had put it together, and it drew admiring comments from Eusebius on the abundance of ecclesiastical correspondence he found in it and was able to exploit for his historical writings. Ever since the second half of the third century, there had been an impressively large collection, over 30,000 volumes, at the church of Caesarea; it was the creation of Pamphilus, a scholarly cleric whose life-long dedication was the amassing of a library of scope and quality. Pamphilus saw to it that it possessed its own scriptorium, which not only took care of the library's needs but produced extra copies of the Bible to lend out or even donate. Eusebius, who was intimate with Pamphilus, was among its users and so was Jerome, probably during his later years when he lived at Bethlehem. The holdings even included some rare books: Jerome mentions a copy of the supposed Hebrew original of the Gospel of Matthew as well as the manuscripts from which Origen made up his Hexapla, his edition of the Old Testament with six versions of the text in parallel columns.

In the west, Rome, despite being the religious capital of the area, had no theological collections of great importance. Its many churches kept just the few books needed for routine activity, such as liturgical manuals and copies of the Scriptures that the lectors used for readings. The papacy at first had only an archive; it was established by Damasus I (366–384), who set it up in the church of San Lorenzo that he had built at his family mansion located near the site occupied today by the Cancelleria. From there sometime later it was transferred to the Lateran Palace, where the papal offices were, and very likely shared its space for the storing of whatever books the papacy acquired. In the course of time these came to include not only Bibles and manuals but a miscellany of Christian theological writings, even some branded as heretical. In a part of the Lateran Palace have been found the remains of a room with a handsome mural, probably of the seventh A.D., showing St. Augustine seated before an open book and holding a roll in one hand. On the basis of this decoration, so suitable for a library, the room has been identified as the place where the papal archives and books were kept.

The papal collection was, so far as we know, strictly Christian. There were mixed feelings among Christian writers about pagan literature. Some of the most influential, such as Augustine and

Jerome, were steeped in the works of Greek and Roman authors, recognized that these were essential models for anyone with aspirations to be a writer, yet were uneasy about them. Was it appropriate for Christians to be exposed to the works of pagans? Jerome gives an account of a troubling dream he had: the heavenly judge appeared to him and asked him what his religious status was. When Jerome answered, "I am a Christian," he was told, "You lie: you are no Christian, you are a Ciceronian." Other churchmen were not merely uneasy but hostile. Pope Gregory the Great (590 to 604), for example, was one such, and very likely saw to it that pagan literature was kept out of the papal holdings.

Yet Rome may have been exceptional in this regard, since collections elsewhere in the west, in Spain for example, included the works of pagan authors. Indeed, the one library whose contents we know in some detail, that of the learned Isidore, bishop of Seville from 600 to 636, had a great many—and this despite the fact that Isidore considered them unfit reading for his monks. Our information about his holdings comes, first and foremost, from a series of verses that he composed to serve as inscriptions on the walls of the library chamber, some over the doors to it and some over the bookcases. The initial verse, no doubt for over the main door, begins with the words: "Here are masses of books, both sacred and secular." And, although the books themselves have disappeared, we can tell from various indications that the statement was no exaggeration. For one, verses that must have been for over bookcases reveal that, besides bookcases for Origen, Eusebius, Chrysostom, Ambrose, Augustine, Jerome, and other such eminent Christian authors, there were bookcases for the Roman jurists Paulus and Gaius and for the Greek medical writers Hippocrates and Galen; for another, quotations from authors and mention of authors' names throughout his works show that he was acquainted with the spectrum of the major Greek and Roman writers. Isidore was no dilettante but a hardworking and serious reader: the last in his series of verses, clearly intended to go over a door, is entitled "To an Intruder" and runs:

When a writer's at work, someone talking aloud he cannot abide.
So, Chatterbox, there's no place for you here. Go on outside!

We do not know what happened to Isidore's books; chances are
they were dispersed and lost. In any event, what contributed to the
survival of Greek and Roman works and was to lead toward the libraries of our times were only in part collections such as his, serving the needs of a learned prelate. They were in even greater part
collections that originated to serve the needs of far more humble
folk—monks.

The institution of monasticism originated in a remote corner of
the eastern empire, the desert of southern Egypt. Sometime in the
first quarter of the fourth century, an Egyptian named Pachomius,
an inspired convert to Christianity, founded in the desert near
Dendyra in Upper Egypt the first monastic community. It was an
immediate success and he quickly planted others nearby; eventually still others, plus some nunneries, arose all over Egypt. Pachomius drew up a code of behavior for his communities and this
has survived in a translation that Jerome made for the benefit of
the devout in the Latin-speaking west. Pachomius, it reveals, insisted that the monks know how to read; the candidates for admis-
sion to his monasteries came mainly from the nearby villages and
no doubt included a large number who were illiterate. A rule in the
code states that whoever among the entrants

> is ignorant of letters, at the first hour and the third and the sixth
> let him go to one who can teach him and who will be assigned to
> him, and he will stand before that man and he will learn with the
> utmost zeal. . . . Even if he is unwilling, he will be compelled to
> read; there will be no one at all in the monastery who does not
> know his letters.

It follows that the monastery had to have books, and a rule concerning them shows how highly they were regarded. There was
a special niche in the wall for storing them, and the second-in-
command at the monastery was charged with taking care of them:
he was to maintain a count of them, and was to lock them up at
night in the niche.

Monastic communities quickly spread throughout the rest of the eastern empire. They had libraries but, so far as we can tell from the available information, which is scanty and late in date, ninth century and after, the libraries were usually small and limited to theological works. The monasteries of Constantinople, for example, probably had collections of no more than one hundred. We have details about one library only, that of the monastery founded in 1088 on the island of Patmos. The founder, Christodoulos, passionately devoted to books, had built up his own extensive library, and this he passed on to the monastery by a bequest at his death. In 1201, as an inventory of that date shows, the total number of books, the original donation plus what had been added through gifts, amounted to 330, which makes it exceptionally large. All but sixteen were theological works.

Yet the eastern empire was a major source of the ancient writings that have survived to our day, especially those in Greek. In all probability most derive from the holdings of the palace and university libraries in Constantinople or of the private collections belonging to the many noted scholars and savants who flourished in the Byzantine Empire. The monasteries of the east played but a minor role in library history. The major role was played by those of the west.

That monks should be able to read was laid down at the outset of monasticism by Pachomius. That they should be made to use this skill, be called upon to read regularly the Scriptures or similar works, was laid down by Benedict in the set of rules he drew up for Monte Cassino, the famous monastery he established in 529 on a towering height roughly midway between Rome and Naples. He stipulates that, in the period from Lent to October, more than half a year, the time from the fourth hour to the sixth the monks should be left free so that they can devote it to reading; from October to Lent, up to the second hour they are to be left free for reading. At the beginning of Lent each monk is to be given a book from the library (*bibliotheca*) which he is to read straight through by the end of Lent; and on Sundays all save those who have assigned duties are to spend the day reading.

The monastery's supply of books, the *bibliotheca* from which the Lenten distribution was made, obviously had to be large enough to furnish a book for each monk, but it probably was not much larger than that. It was, furthermore, almost certainly limited to Bibles and other basic religious works. Where did its supply come from? There is no indication of the existence of a scriptorium, the feature that will be so important in the monasteries of later centuries. Quite possibly some books were gifts—but this simply begs the question: where did the benefactors get them? Probably from booksellers, just as most seekers of books had in pre-Christian times; and booksellers may well have been where Benedict's *bibliotheca* got desiderata that hadn't been received as gifts. For the spread of Christianity did not put booksellers out of business; it simply added religious works to what they offered for sale. How lively their trade was is revealed in an anecdote told by Sulpicius Severus, a Roman aristocrat who converted to Christianity and around 400 wrote a biography of his contemporary, St. Martin of Tours. Severus reports that, when a copy of his work arrived at Rome, "since all in the city were competing to get their hands on it, I saw the booksellers exulting that it was the greatest source of profit they had, nothing sold faster, nothing sold for a better price." Two centuries later Rome was still a center of the trade: in 596 Pope Gregory established a mission in Britain and the books it was equipped with came from Rome. The books were necessarily supplied by dealers, since no religious institutions in the city at the time had scriptoria. There were other good places for buying books besides Rome: not long after Benedict's establishment of Monte Cassino, Cassiodorus founded a monastery where great emphasis was placed on learning and literature, and he purchased much of what he needed for its library from northern Africa.

Cassiodorus is a key figure in library history. The monastery he brought into existence was unusual—as we might expect of an unusual man, one who was a politician, statesman, intellectual, and author before he decided to devote his life to religion. He came from a family of note. His father had held high office in the government of Italy, and Cassiodorus followed in his footsteps. Until he was of middle age he was in government service and rose to the upper levels. Then, sometime around 540 or 550, he abandoned public life and on his ancestral estate near Squillace in southern Italy he set about creating his idea of a model monastery. He called it Vivarium after the ponds for raising fish (*vivaria*) that were nearby. During his career as official and statesman, he had found time to pursue intellectual interests that embraced all aspects of knowledge; he now sought to institute a monastic life that encompassed breadth of knowledge along with religion. He composed a book for the benefit of his monks, the *Institutiones,* in which he ranged over sacred and secular literature and dwelled upon the art of the copyist of manuscripts, emphasizing how great is its importance, how demanding are its requirements. Monasteries from the beginning had employed some of their monks as scribes, but only to take care of the routine paperwork; it was considered a lowly activity and assigned to the younger members or to those unfit for higher duties. To Cassiodorus it counted as one of the highest possible activities: in his eyes, the monk who is trained as a scribe for the copying of manuscripts of Holy Writ "with his hand preaches to men, with his fingers loosens their tongues, without speaking gives salvation to mortals, with pen and ink fights against the unlawful temptations of the devil." Cassiodorus did not limit his enthusiasm for copying to theological works; he would have his monks copy secular literature as well. He was a stickler about accuracy, even writing a treatise, *De Orthographia,* in which he presents the rules of spelling so that his copyists could avoid committing certain common errors.

Cassiodorus saw to it that Vivarium had a library that would make possible the ample knowledge he wanted his monks to acquire. He started it by donating his own books, and he filled in gaps by purchases; the scriptorium was able to turn out as many copies as were needed. The collection included, beyond the full representation of Christian writings, almost all the major pagan Latin authors and, of Greek, Homer, Aristotle, Plato, Hippocrates, Galen, and others.

Cassiodorus was Vivarium's guiding spirit. He died sometime

between 575 and 585, in his nineties, and soon after his departure from the scene the monastery ceased to exist. What he believed in, that the copying of manuscripts was a lofty activity for monks to carry on and that a monastery library should have range and depth, was kept alive by his *Institutiones,* which came to be widely owned, by individuals as well as monasteries. Monastery libraries, since their original reason for being was to supply monks with reading matter for spiritual benefit, at the outset were mere in-house lending libraries stocked with a narrow selection of works; under the influence of the *Institutiones* they gradually moved toward becoming research libraries. They set up scriptoria and resorted to interlibrary loan to expand their holdings, borrowing titles they wanted from monasteries that owned them and having the scriptorium make copies.

In 612, less than half a century after Cassiodorus' death, St. Columban founded a monastery at Bobbio near Pavia that included a scriptorium and a library, both of which quickly grew to be important features of the institution. The same happened elsewhere as time went on, at St. Gallen in Switzerland, Fulda in Germany, and a good number of other places. We owe to the holdings amassed in such monasteries most of what has survived of the writings in Latin and Greek from the ancient world, particularly in Latin. From the monasteries the manuscripts passed in various ways—copying, gift, sale, theft, looting—to form the core of important libraries of the late Middle Ages and the Renaissance. These libraries, whether founded by scholars who gloried in reading books, such as Petrarch, or by nobles who gloried in collecting them, such as the Medici family, mark the opening of a new age of library history.

Abbreviations

AJA:	*American Journal of Archaeology*
AJPh:	*American Journal of Philology*
Blanchard:	A. Blanchard, ed., *Les débuts du codex* (Turnhout 1989)
Blum:	R. Blum, *Kallimachos: The Alexandrian Library and the Beginnings of Bibliography,* trans. H. Wellisch (Madison 1991)
BCH:	*Bulletin de Correspondance Hellénique*
CAH:	*Cambridge Ancient History*
Callmer:	C. Callmer, "Antiken Bibliotheken," *Skrifter utgivna av Svenska Institutet I Rom* 10 (Opuscula Archaeologica 3, Lund 1944) 145–193
CIL:	*Corpus Inscriptionum Latinarum*
Fehrle:	R. Fehrle, *Das Bibliothekswesen im alten Rom* (Wiesbaden 1986)
Fraser:	P. Fraser, *Ptolemaic Alexandria* (Oxford 1972)
GRBS:	*Greek, Roman, and Byzantine Studies*
Harris:	W. Harris, *Ancient Literacy* (Cambridge 1989)
IG:	*Inscriptiones Graecae*
ILS:	H. Dessau, *Inscriptiones Latinae Selectae* (Berlin 1892–1916)
JHS:	*Journal of Hellenic Studies*
Leclercq:	"Bibliothèques" in F. Cabrol and H. Leclercq, *Dictionnaire d'archéologie chrétienne et de liturgie* ii (Paris 1925) 842–904
Lewis:	N. Lewis, *Papyrus in Classical Antiquity* (Oxford 1974)
LSJ:	H. Liddell, R. Scott, H. Jones, *A Greek-English Lexicon*
MDAI (A) (R):	*Mitteilungen des kaiserlich deutschen archäologischen Instituts (Athenische Abteilung) (Römische Abteilung)*

Nash: E. Nash, *Pictorial Dictionary of Ancient Rome* (New York 1968²)

OCD: *Oxford Classical Dictionary*

Oppenheim: L. Oppenheim, *Ancient Mesopotamia* (Chicago 1977²)

Packer: J. Packer, *The Forum of Trajan in Rome* (Berkeley 1997)

Parpola: S. Parpola, "Assyrian Library Records," *Journal of Near Eastern Studies* 42 (1983) 1–29

Pfeiffer: R. Pfeiffer, *History of Classical Scholarship* (Oxford 1968)

Pflaum: H. Pflaum, *Les carrières procuratoriennes équestres sous le haut-empire romain* (Paris 1960–1961)

Platthy: J. Platthy, *Sources on the Earliest Greek Libraries* (Amsterdam 1968)

Pliny, *N.H.*: Pliny the Elder, *Historia Naturalis*

RE: *Paulys Real-Encyclopädie der classischen Altertumswissenschaft*

REG: *Revue des études grecques*

Roberts-Skeat: C. Roberts and T. Skeat, *The Birth of the Codex* (London 1983)

Strocka: V. Strocka, "Römische Bibliotheken," *Gymnasium* 88 (1981) 298–329

Syll.:   W. Dittenberger, *Sylloge Inscriptionum Graecarum* (Leipzig 1917³)

TAPA: *Transactions of the American Philological Association*

Thompson: J. Thompson, *The Medieval Library* (Chicago 1939)

Turner: E. Turner, *Greek Papyri: An Introduction* (Oxford 1980)

van Haelst: J. van Haelst, "Les origines du codex," in Blanchard 13–35

Veenhof: K. Veenhof, ed., *Cuneiform Archives and Libraries*. Papers read at the 30ᵉ rencontre Assyriologique Internationale, Leiden, 4–8 July 1983 (Istanbul 1986)

Weaver: P. Weaver, *Familia Caesaris* (Cambridge 1972)

Weitemeyer: M. Weitemeyer, "Archive and Library Technique in Ancient Mesopotamia," *Libri* 6 (1956) 217–238

Wilson: N. Wilson, "The Libraries of the Byzantine World," *GRBS* 8 (1967) 53–80

Notes

A superscript number following a title or year of publication indicates the edition.

Chapter 1. The Beginnings: *The Ancient Near East*

Page

1–4 Writing: *CAH*³ i.2, 90, 93–96; Weitemeyer 219. Clay tablets: Veenhof in Veenhof 1–2; Oppenheim 228–229, 239–240. Akkadian use of cuneiform: *CAH*³ i.2, 450–451.Archives and non-archival materials: Veenhof in Veenhof 4–11. Early lists from near Nippur: R. Biggs in *Journal of Cuneiform Studies* 20.2 (1966) 73–88. Ebla: P. Matthiae in Veenhof 53–71, esp. 64; A. Archi in Veenhof 72–86, esp. 77–83. Nippur catalogue: Weitemeyer 231–232.

4–7 Hattusas: H. Otten in *Das Altertum* 1 (1955) 71–81. Colophons: Oppenheim 240–241; Weitemeyer 226–227. Colophons at Hattusas: Otten 76–77. Hattusas catalogue: Otten 74–76; E. Laroche in *Archiv Orientální* 17.2 (1949) 7–23, esp. 15–20. Catalogue entry same as a colophon: Laroche 17 (No. xxviii, lines 19–24). Incongruous entry: Otten 75–76. Palace holdings: O. Gurney, *The Hittites* (Penguin 1952) 143–161.

8–9 More than one hundred titles: based on the number of texts listed in Laroche (op. cit. under **4–7** above) 14–22. Training of scribes: Oppenheim 14. Personal libraries: 243; Veenhof in Veenhof 5. Absence of book trade: Cf. Parpola 10. Tiglath-Pileser's library: E. Weidner in *Archiv für Orientforschung* 16 (1952–1953) 197–211. Catalogue of hymns: S. Langdon in *Journal of the Royal Asiatic Society* (1921) 169–191, esp. 170–171 ("5 Sumerian psalms"), 173 ("Song to the reed flute," "Three recitations").

9–12 "Has every right": Oppenheim 15. "the highest level," "among the kings": M. Streck, *Assurbanipal und die letzten* *assyrischen Könige bis zum Untergange Niniveh's.* ii, *Texte* (Leipzig 1916) 356–357, No. c, lines 4–6; cf. S. Lieberman in T. Abusch et al., eds., *Lingering over Words: Studies in Ancient Near Eastern Literature in Honor of William L. Moran* (Atlanta 1990) 319. Finds at Nineveh: J. Reade in Veenhof 213–222. Ashurbanipal's colophons: Weitemeyer 228. Composition of Ashurbanipal's library: Oppenheim 16–17; C. Walker in F. Fales and B. Hickey, eds., *Austen Henry Layard tra l'Oriente e Venezia* (Rome 1987) 188. 1,500 titles, numerous copies: Oppenheim 17–18. Tablets from Babylon, from Tiglath-Pileser's collection: Weidner (op. cit. under **8–9** above) 198, 204. Accession record: Parpola 1–29. "2 lamentations": 14. "1 one-column": 18. Turned over disposable holdings: 8–9. Size of acquisition: 4. Use of wood boards: 8.

12–14 Colophon with threat: Streck (op. cit. under **9–12** above) 358–359, No. e. Similar threats: Nos. b, c, f. "Whoever opens": R. Thompson, *The Reports of the Magicians and Astrologers of Nineveh and Babylon in the British Museum* (London 1900) vol. 2, p. lix, No. 152. Library ills of private collections: G. Offner in *Revue d'assyriologie et d'archéologie orientale* 44 (1950) 135–143. Borrowing: Offner 142. Not to leave the premises: 140. Simple caution: 142. No rubbing out of text: 138. The wrath of every god: Offner 137; Weitemeyer 230. Carry off by theft, fraud: Offner 139–140. Carry him off: 140. "He who carries off this tablet": 136. "He who steals it by theft": 137. Tablet in the temple: 141.

14–16 "A reference library geared": Oppenheim 20. Geared to one specific need: Lieberman (op. cit. under **9–12** above) 316–321, 327–329. Epic of Creation and the New Year: Oppenheim 178. Epic of Irra and plague: 235. Atrahasis and childbirth: E. Reiner and H. Güterbock in *Journal of Cuneiform Studies* 21 (1967) 257. Egyptian libraries: F. Milkau in *Handbuch der Bibliothekswissenschaft* 3.1 (Wiesbaden 1955) 6–16. "Ozymandias": Diodorus 1.49.3.

Chapter 2. The Beginning: *Greece*

17–18 Mycenaean Writing: *CAH*[3] ii.1, 599–560. Greek alphabet: *CAH*[3] iii.1, 819–833.

19–21   Widespread literacy: F. Harvey in *REG* 79 (1966) 585–635,
        L. Woodbury in *TAPA* 106 (1976) 349–357, A. Burns in
        Journal of the History of Ideas 42 (1981) 371–387, S. Stod-
        dard and J. Whitley in *Antiquity* 62 (1988) 761–772. Lim-
        ited literacy: Harris 93–115, esp. 114–115; R. Thomas, *Oral
        Tradition and Written Record in Classical Athens* (Cambridge
        1989) 15–34, who emphasizes the importance of oral com-
        munication. Euripides' *Theseus:* Athenaeus 10.454b–c.
        Odyssey committed to writing ca. 550 B.C.: G. Nagy in *TAPA*
        122 (1992) 52. Greek vase-paintings: J. Beazley in *AJA* 52
        (1948) 336–340. Sappho: Beazley 339. Schools: Harris 96–
        102. On Chios: Herodotus 6.27.2; on Astypalaea: Pausanias
        6.9.6–7; at Mycalessus: Thucydides 7.29.5. Tombstone
        from Athens: G. Richter in *MDAI (A)* 71 (1956) 141–144.
        Literacy of women: S. Cole in H. Foley, ed., *Reflections of
        Women in Antiquity* (New York 1981) 219–245, esp. 223–
        227; Harris 106–108. Heraclitus, Hecataeus: E. Turner,
        Athenian Books in the Fifth and Fourth Centuries B.C. (London
        1952) 17–18.

21–24   Herodotus wrote for readers: cf. S. Flory in *AJPh* 101
        (1980) 14. "squeezed out of books": *Frogs* 943. "even if the
        man": 1407–1409. "When they know": Plato, *Protagoras*
        325e. Handbooks: Cf. Turner (op. cit. under **19–21** above)
        18. Sophocles: *Suda* s.v. "Sophocles." Agatharchus: Vitru-
        vius 7, praef. 11. Polyclitus: Cf. *OCD*³ s.v. "Polyclitus." Icti-
        nus: Vitruvius 7, praef. 12. Menaecus: Plato, *Gorgias* 518b.
        Ostracism: *OCD*³ s.v. "ostracism." Use of skins by peoples of
        Near East and nearby Greeks: Lewis 8–9.

25–26   Habitat of papyrus: Lewis 3–20. Earliest papyrus paper and
        export: 84. Manufacture: 34–69; *OCD*³ 250. Number of
        sheets to a roll, length of rolls: N. Lewis, *Papyrus in Classical
        Antiquity: A Supplement* (Papyrologica Bruxellensia 23,
        Brussels 1989) 26. Reed pens: Turner 10.

27–28   Booksellers: See *LSJ* s.v. βιβλιοπώλης, where citations from
        writers of the fifth and fifth/fourth centuries are given.
        "where books are for sale": Eupolis, cited by Pollux (9.47);
        cf. Lewis 74. "a possession": Thucydides 1.22.4. Absence of
        author's rights: Cf. B. Van Groningen in *Mnemosyne* 16
        (1963) 1–17, esp. 7. Anaxagoras' works: Plato, *Apologia*

26d, and cf. Lewis 74. Wages: H. Michell, *The Economics of Ancient Greece* (New York 1957²) 131. Zeno: Diogenes Laertius 7.31. Plato's disciple (Hermodorus): Zenobius 5.6 and cf. van Groningen 10–11. Aristophanes pokes fun: Aristophanes very likely had a library of his own that included the bulk of Euripides' works; see N. Lowe in *Annals of Scholarship* 10 (1993) 73–74. Library of would-be savant (Euthydemus): Xenophon, *Memorabilia* 4.2.1, 10. Linus: Athenaeus 4.164c.

29–30 Aristotle's library: Strabo 13.609. Aristotle's collection and the Alexandrian library: Athenaeus (1.3a) states that Aristotle's collection was purchased by Ptolemy II and brought to Alexandria but Strabo, whose account of what happened to it is more trustworthy, makes no mention of this. Demetrius of Phalerum: Some not very reliable sources state that he helped Ptolemy II assemble the collection and served as its first head, but this contradicts what is known about his life. After leaving Athens he went to Alexandria and became a close associate of the first Ptolemy. See Pfeiffer 103–104, Fraser 314–315, 321–322. Lycurgus' decree: Plutarch, *Moralia* 841f.

Chapter 3. The Library of Alexandria

31–33 The struggle over Alexander's empire: W. Tarn and G. Griffith, *Hellenistic Civilisation* (London 1952³) 5–11. Ptolemy I, a historian: Pfeiffer 95–96. "royal road": Fraser 386. Ptolemy II a zoologist: Fraser iia, 466, n. 39. Ptolemy III patron of letters: Pfeiffer 102, Fraser 306–307. Ptolemy IV a playwright: Fraser 311. Tutors: Zenodotus and Strato tutored Ptolemy II (Pfeiffer 92), Apollonius Rhodius Ptolemy III (Fraser 331), Eratosthenes probably Ptolemy IV (Pfeiffer 124).

33–34 Euclid and Strato invitees of Ptolemy I: Fraser 386–387, 427. Eratosthenes invitee of Ptolemy III: Pfeiffer 124. Herophilus at Alexandria: Fraser 348. Archimedes at Alexandria: 309. The Museum: 312–319. "scribbling bookworms": Athenaeus 1.22d. Library: Fraser 321–325.

34–37 Acquisition methods: Fraser 325–326. Accessions procedure: 326–327. Inclusion of translations: 330. Ptolemy II promotes classics: 449. Disorder in texts of Homer: Pfeiffer 109–110. Copies from Chios, Argos, Sinope: Fraser 328. Size of holdings: 328–329. Office of Director: 322. Zenodotus first director: 330.

37–38   Zenodotus' organization: Blum 226–230. Zenodotus' glossary: Pfeiffer 115. Alphabetization: Blum 191–192. Aristophanes of Byzantium anecdote: Vitruvius 7 Praef. 5–7.

38–41   Callimachus' life: Blum 126. Cataloguer of the library: 230. *Pinakes:* Pfeiffer 128–129, Fraser 452–453. "miscellaneous table": Blum 154. Biographical sketches: 152–153. Plays of Aeschylus, Euripides: 190–191. List of Theophrastus' works: 59–61. Well-nigh all: The library lacked a few works that had perished before its creation (Fraser 329–330). Eratosthenes' directorship: Fraser 332. *Beta:* Pfeiffer 170.

41–43   Eratosthenes' geographical works: Fraser 525–538. Directorship of Aristophanes, Aristarchus: 332–333. Their editions of texts: 459–460, 462–463. Aristarchus' commentaries: Pfeiffer 212–213. On Herodotus: 224–225.

43–45   Philitas: Pfeiffer 88–90. Scene from comedy: cited in Athenaeus 9.382c; cf. Pfeiffer 91. Aristophanes' *Lexeis:* Pfeiffer 197–202. *melygion* etc.: B. Grenfell and A. Hunt, *The Oxyrhynchus Papyri* xv (London 1922) no. 1802. Didymus: Pfeiffer 274–278. Dionysius Thrax: 266–272.

45–47   Library destroyed: Fraser 334–335, Blum 99. Merely damaged: Tarn and Griffith (op. cit. under **31–33** above) 270, D. Delia in *American Historical Review* 97 (1992) 1461–1462. "being cut off from his ships": Plutarch, *Caesar* 49. "many places": Dio Cassius 42.38.2. Antony's gift: Plutarch, *Antony* 58–59. Directorship to political figures: Fraser 333–334. "Honorary" Museum memberships: N. Lewis, *On Government and Law in Roman Egypt* (Atlanta 1995) 262–266. Balbillus: Pflaum i 34–41. Destruction during Aurelian's campaign: Ammianus Marcellinus 22.16.15; cf. Delia 1463.

Chapter 4. The Growth of Libraries

48–49   Library at Antioch: Pfeiffer 122. Euphorion: 150. Philetaerus: E. Hansen, *The Attalids of Pergamon* (Ithaca 1972²)

14–19. Attalus as patron of arts and art collector: 301–306, 316. Eumenes founds library: Pfeiffer 235, Fraser 465. Aristotle's books: Strabo 13.608–609 (Aristotle bequeathed his collection to Theophrastus, his successor as head of his school; Theophrastus bequeathed it, along with his own library, to Neleus, a disciple; Neleus brought it to his hometown Scepsis, which was in Pergamene territory; there it passed to his heirs, "ordinary people" who never used the books but kept them locked up until rumors of the king's zeal for acquisitions scared them into burying them).

49–53 Archaeological remains of the library: Callmer 148–153; see W. Radt, *Pergamon: Geschichte und Bauten einer antiken Metropole* (Darmstadt 1999) 165–168, for a review of recent suggestions, mostly unconvincing, for the arrangement and location of the library. *Pinakes* of Pergamene library: Pfeiffer 133–134. Imprisonment of Aristophanes: Pfeiffer 172, Fraser 461. "because of the rivalry": Pliny, *N.H.* 13.70. Use of leather as writing material: Pfeiffer 236. "the kings of Alexandria": Pliny, *N.H.* 35.10. Crates' teachings: Fraser 465–466. "he fell into": Suetonius, *De Gram. et Rhet.* 2.

53–54 Desirability of universal education: Cf. Harris 130. "passed a law": Diodorus 12.12.4. Teos inscription: *Syll.*[3] 578.2–13. Miletus inscription: *Syll.*[3] 577.4–5, 50–53. An inscription found at Pergamum dating to the third or second century B.C. indicates that girls there must have been included in the educational system since it records contests in school subjects (reading, calligraphy) in which they took part; *MDAI (A)* 35 (1910) 436, 37 (1912) 277–278. Eumenes' donation to Rhodes: Polybius 31.31.1. Attalus' donation to Delphi: *Syll.*[3] 672.4, 7–9, 24. Other benefactions: Harris 131–132. Ptolemies' exemption: 132. Much higher level of literacy: 141.

54–56 Finds of papyrus documents: Turner, Chap. 2. Ptolemaic bureaucracy: *CAH* vii[2].1, 145–154 (a discussion that emphasizes its shortcomings). "If you have already": C. Edgar, *Zenon Papyri* iv (Cairo 1931) No. 59588.3–5. Hellenistic literary papyri: O. Montevecchi, *La Papirologia* (Turin 1973) 360–363; W. Willis in *GRBS* 9 (1968) 217. Literary finds in villages: Turner 81. Homer, Euripides: Turner 97. Used as school texts: Montevecchi 396. *Iliad* ii found with mummy: Turner 77. Timotheus papyrus: 32. Writings of various kinds: See the listings in Montevecchi 360–363. Technical manuals: Harris 127.

56–57   Write them out themselves: For a possible instance of a village clerk writing out passages of Greek poetry, see N. Lewis, *Greeks in Ptolemaic Egypt* (Oxford 1986) 122–123. Homer available in bookstores: Papyrus texts of Homer that date before 150 B.C. contain many spurious lines, whereas those after this date do not. It has been suggested that the change was due to the copy shops and booksellers, who became aware of the spurious lines through the studies of the Alexandrian savants and discovered that editions without them found favor with buyers; see P. Collart in *Revue de Philologie et d'Histoire Ancienne* 59 (1933) 53–54; S. West, *The Ptolemaic Papyri of Homer* (Papyrologica Coloniensia iii, 1967) 17. Supplying paper to copy shops: Cf. Turner 95. Sources of copies to work from: L. Canfora, in G. Cavallo, ed., *Le biblioteche nel mondo antico e medievale* (Bari 1988) 15, suggests for Alexandria the library in the temple of Serapis since it would have been easier of access than the great library of the Museum. Aristotle's *Constitution of Athens:* Turner 96.

57–59   Cos inscription: *BCH* 59 (1935) 421–425. Libraries elsewhere: A library is attested at Mylasa in Asia Minor in the third century B.C. (Platthy no. 136). The gymnasium: See *OCD³* s.v. "gymnasium." *Ptolemaion* inscriptions: Platthy nos. 28–35. *Iliad* and Euripides: Platthy no. 33 (= *IG* ii² 1041). Duplicates or replacements: Cf. M. Tod in *JHS* 77 (1977) 139. Another inscription: Platthy no. 90 (= *IG* ii² 2363); see also E. Burzachechi, *Rendiconti della Accademia Nazionale dei Lincei, Classe di Scienze morali, storiche e filologiche* 18 (1963) 93–96. Record of donations: First suggested by U. Wilamowitz, *Analecta Euripidea* (Berlin 1875) 141, and generally approved; see Blum 191, Tod 139.

59–60   Rhodes inscription: M. Segre, *Rivista di filologia e d'istruzione classica* 13 (1935) 214–222 = Platthy no. 117; see also Blum 185–187. Another inscription: Segre 219 = Platthy no. 119. Cities with gymnasiums: *RE* s.v. "gymnasium" 2005.

Chapter 5. The Beginnings: *Rome*

61–62   Latin alphabet: *OCD*³ s.v. "alphabets of Italy." Earliest Latin writings: Harris 151–155. Livius: *OCD*³ s.v. "Livius Andronicus;" W. Beare, *The Roman Stage* (New York 1965³) 27–29. Horace read Livius: *Epistulae* 2.1.70–71.

62–64   Plautus: *OCD*³ s.v. "Plautus;" G. Duckworth, *The Nature of Roman Comedy* (Princeton 1952) 49–56. Staging of Roman plays: Beare (op. cit. under **61–62** above) 163–166. Fifty known plays: Duckworth 52. Sources: *OCD*³ 1195. Reduced to turning a millstone: Gellius 3.3.14. Theater managers: Beare 164–165. "out to lay away cash": *Epistulae* 2.1.175–176.

65–66   Roman philhellenism: *OCD*³ s.v. "philhellenism," esp. p. 1160. Scipio: *OCD*³ s.v. "Cornelius Scipio Aemilianus." Quotes Homer: Appian, *Punica* 132; Scipio quotes the prophetic words that Hector speaks to his wife: "There will come a day when sacred Ilion shall perish, / and Priam and the people of Priam of the strong ash spear" (*Il.* 6.448–449; trans. R. Lattimore). Macedonian library: Plutarch, *Aemilius Paulus* 28.6. Nature of the library: Cf. E. Rawson in *CAH* viii² 464. Ennius: *OCD*³ s.v. "Ennius, Quintus." Euhemerus: *OCD*³ s.v. "Euhemerus."

66–67   "The one among": Cicero, *Brutus* 20.78. Explains eclipse: Livy 44.37. Book on eclipses: Pliny, *N.H.* 2.53. Aratus: *OCD*³ s.v. "Aratus (1)." Polybius: *OCD*³ s.v. "Polybius." "where Timaeus left off": Polybius 1.5.1. Theopompus: 8.9–11. Phylarchus: 2.56.1–8. Philinus: 1.14.1–3. Chaereas and Sosylus: 3.20.5. Aratus: 2.40.4.

68–69   Sulla's library, Tyrannio, Apellicon: Strabo 13.609. Lucullus' library: Isidore, *Etymologiae* 6.5.1. "What Lucullus did": Plutarch, *Luc.* 42.1.

70   Atticus' fluency in Greek: Nepos, *Att.* 4.1. Varro: *OCD*³ s.v. "Varro." His works: *RE* Suppl. 6 (1938), p. 1180. Fifty authorities: *De re rustica* 1.8–10.

70–72   Cicero's letters: D. Shackleton Bailey, ed., *Cicero's Letters to Atticus* (Cambridge 1965–1970), *Ad Familiares* (1977), *Ad Quintum Fratrem* (1980). White-collar work: Even Tiro, Cicero's highly esteemed chief secretary and an author of books himself, was a slave whom Cicero did not manumit until late in his life (see *OCD*[3] s.v. "Tullius Tiro"); Atticus' slaves included *plurimi librarii* "very many copyists" (Nepos, *Atticus* 13.3). Copying a major part of their work: cf. *Att.* 13.21a.2, where Cicero, in eliminating the possibility that his people had made two copies of his *De Finibus*, remarks that "they barely finished one." "you will see": Cicero, *Att.* 4.4a.1. "My slave Dionysius": *Ad Fam.* 13.77.3. "I'm told that": *Ad Fam.* 5.9.2. "About your Dionysius": *Ad Fam.* 5.10a.1.

73–75   Borrowing from Atticus: E.g., on 27 February 49 B.C. Cicero asked to borrow Demetrius' *On Concord* (*Att.* 8.11.7), repeats the request on 28 February (8.12.6), and by 17 March has returned the book (9.9.2). For other loan requests, see R. Sommer in *Hermes* 61 (1926) 398. "write home to Rome": *Att.* 4.14.1; Cicero was doing research for his *De Republica* at the time (May 54 B.C.). Books requested when at a villa: E.g., in *Att.* 13.31.2 and 13.32.2, written from Tusculum, he requests certain books by Dicaearchus (a pupil of Aristotle, who wrote on a wide range of subjects). Used Sulla's library: *Att.* 4.10.1, and cf. E. Rawson, *Intellectual Life in the Late Roman Republic* (Baltimore 1985) 41, for what is surely the right explanation for Cicero's expression, "I am feeding on Faustus' library." "when I was at my place": *De Finibus* 3.2.7. Villa library at Herculaneum: Callmer 155–156; J. Deiss, *Herculaneum: Italy's Buried Treasure* (New York 1966) 54–56.

76–77   "I am very grateful": *Att.* 2.4.1. Serapion: *RE* s.v. "Serapion (4)." "The geographical work": *Att.* 2.6.1. Hipparchus: *OCD*[3] s.v. "Hipparchus (3)." Alexander of Ephesus: Strabo 14.642. "I have received": *Att.* 2.20.6. "I am returning": *Att.* 2.22.7.

77–78   Acquiring of books: See R. Starr in *Classical Quarterly* 37 (1987) 213–219. Copies in the public domain: 215. Caerellia's surreptitious copying: *Att.* 13.21a.2. Tullia: Cicero ap. Lactantius, *Institutiones Divinae* 1.15.20. Atticus' daughter: Suetonius, *Gramm.* 16. Pompey's daughter: Plutarch, *Moralia* 737B. Pompey's wife: Plutarch, *Pompey* 55.

78–79   *taberna libraria:* Cicero, *Philippicae* 2.9.21. Atticus' copy of

Serapion: Cicero acknowledges receipt in early April 59 B.C. (the date of *Att.* 2.4), and Atticus had been in Rome since at least December 60 (the date of *Att.* 2.2, sent to Atticus in Rome). "For books in Latin": *Ad Quint. Frat.* 3.5.6. "used incompetent scribes": Strabo 13.609. Bring an expert, Tyrannio: *Ad Quint. Frat.* 3.4.5. "the books one would like": ibid. One of Cicero's first collections: In *Att.* 1.7, written from Rome in February 67 B.C., he reminds Atticus of the promise "to put together a library for me." "I am saving": *Att.* 1.10.4, written in May 67. In *Att.* 1.11.3, written in August 67, and in 1.4.3, written in the first half of 66, he still has not collected the funds and pleads with Atticus not to dispose of the books elsewhere.

79   "to build for public use": Suet., *Caes.* 44. Asinius Pollio: Isidore, *Etymologiae* 6.5.2.

Chapter 6. Libraries of the Roman Empire: *The City of Rome*

80   Pollio: *OCD*³ s.v. "Asinius Pollio, Gaius." His library: Isidore, *Etymologiae* 6.5.2. Its location: Cf. Callmer 156–157. Statue of Varro: Pliny, *N.H.* 7.115.

81–83   Augustus' libraries: Suetonius, *Augustus* 29.3 (Palatine); Plutarch, *Marcellus* 30.6 and Dio Cassius 49.43.8 (Porticus of Octavia). Two sections in library of Porticus of Octavia: See *CIL* 6.4433, 4435. Remains of Palatine Library: Strocka 307–309. Eighteen bookcases: See the reconstruction in Strocka 308, fig. 4. *armaria:* See, e.g., Pliny, *Epistulae* 2.17.8 and *Digest* 32.52.3, and cf. Callmer 188. Bookcases numbered: See Scriptores Historiae Augustae, *Tacitus* 8.1, where mention is made of a book "in the sixth bookcase in Trajan's library" (*in bibliotheca Ulpia in armario sexto*); it is a reasonable assumption that the system of numbering the bookcases was common to all the imperial libraries. Colonnade nearby: Cf. the plan in Nash i 204. Roman innovation: Cf. Callmer 159, 188; Strocka 308, who suggests that the Palatine Library was the first example.

84   Tiberius' library: Pliny (*N.H.* 34.43) mentions a *bibliotheca templi Augusti* and Gellius (13.20.1) a *domus Tiberianae bibliotheca*. They may refer to the same library; cf. *RE* s.v. "Bibliotheken" 418. Vespasian's library: Gellius 16.8.2. On the possible identification of its remains, see Callmer 161–162. Fifty-foot statue: Suetonius, *Tiberius* 74; Pliny, *N.H.* 34.43.

84–88 Trajan's library: Packer i 450–454.

88–89 Decoration of bookcases: Cf. Seneca, *De tranquilitate animi* 9.6 (mention of "*armaria* of citrus and of ivory"). Roman baths: J. Carcopino, *Daily Life in Ancient Rome*, trans. E. Lorimer, ed. H. Rowell (New Haven 1940) 254–263. "What worse than Nero": Martial 7.34.4–5. Remains of Baths of Nero: Nash ii 460–464.

89–91 Baths of Trajan: Strocka 311–313; Nash ii 472–477, esp. 476, fig. 1290. Baths of Caracalla: Strocka 315–316; Nash ii 434–441, esp. 438, fig. 1237. Baths of Diocletian: Nash ii 448–453.

92 Burning and restoration of the Palatine Library: Callmer 157–159; Strocka 307–308. Of the Library of the Porticus of Octavia: Dio Cassius 66.24.2; Suetonius, *Domitian* 20. Of the library in the Temple of Peace: Dio Cassius 73.24.1–2; Ammianus Marcellinus 16.10.14 (where he lists the temple as one of the city's sights in 357). Trajan's library in 456: Sidonius Apollinaris, *Carmina* 8.7–8 and *Epistulae* 9.16.2, lines 25–28.

93 Macer: Pflaum i 11–13 (Pflaum mistakenly assumes that Macer was a director of the libraries. He was simply in charge of setting up the Palatine Library; see Fehrle 75–76). Melissus: Suetonius, *De Gram. et Rhet.* 21 and cf. *RE* s.v. "Melissus, C. Maecenas." Hyginus: Suetonius, *De Gram. et Rhet.* 20 and cf. *RE* s.v. "(C.) Iulius Hyginus."

94–95 Pappus: *AJA* 63 (1959) 384 and cf. the entry in *Prosopographia Imperii Romani, Saec. I, II, III*, Pars iv (Berlin 1952–1956²), no. 447, where Pappus is identified as a freedman; S. Panciera argues (*Epigraphica* 31 [1969] 112–120, esp. 113), probably rightly, that he must be of free birth, probably a Greek who had recently acquired Roman citizenship. "an intimate": the Latin is *comes*, on which see Panciera 113–114. Scirtus: *CIL* 10.1739 = *ILS* 1587. "freedman of Augustus": Cf. Weaver 51. *familia Caesaris:* Weaver 2. Range of duties: 7. Procuratorship as culmination of a career: 267–281.

95–96   Dionysius: Pflaum i 111–112. Salaries: H. Pflaum, *Les procu-
rateurs équestres sous le haut-empire romain* (Paris 1950) 236–
237. Eudaemon: Pflaum i 264–271. Philosopher: L. Julius
Vestinus; see Pflaum i 245–247. Jurist: L. Volusius Mae-
cianus; see Pflaum i 333–336. Suetonius: For his career in
public service, see Pflaum i 219–224 and *OCD*[3] 1451.

97–98   Aurelius' letter: Fronto, *Epistulae* 4.5.2. Antiochus: *CIL*
6.5884; for other slaves in the Latin section of the Palatine
Library, see 6.5189, 6.5191 and, for a slave in the Greek
section, see 6.5188. Laryx: *CIL* 6.4433; for a slave in the
Latin section of the Library of the Porticus of Octavia, see
6.4431. Montanus: *CIL* 6.4435. Onesimus: 6.8679.
Hymenaeus: 6.8907.

99–102   Ovid's lament: *Tristia* 3.1.59–72. "He came close to banning": *Caligula* 34.2. "Sent a short": *Iulius* 56.7. Lists their
titles: They included a poem "In Praise of Hercules" and a
tragedy "Oedipus." Gellius: *OCD*[3] s.v. "Gellius, Aulus."
"Made a painstaking search": 16.8.2. "Many of the letters":
5.21.9. For the two writers mentioned, see *OCD*[3] s.v.
"Aelius, Lucius" and s.v. "Sinnius Capito." Edicts of praetors: Gellius 11.17.1. "He enshrined": Suetonius, *Tiberius*
70.2. Greek medical treatise: *Anthologia Palatina* 7.158; the
author was Marcellus of Side (cf. *OCD*[3] s.v. "Marcellus").

102–103   Mark of status: Cf. N. Horsfall in *Greece & Rome* 40 (1993)
61–62. Confiscations: Varro's villa with his library was
plundered by Mark Antony; Lucullus' library had been inherited by his son, who was killed at Philippi in 42 B.C.
fighting on the side of Brutus and Cassius; Sulla's had been
inherited by his son Faustus, who was killed fighting
against Caesar in Africa in 46 B.C. Atticus' death: Cf.
R. Syme, *The Roman Revolution* (Oxford 1939) 257.
"collected copies": *Domitian* 20.

103–105   Book trade in imperial times: Cf. R. Starr in *Classical Quarterly* 37 (1987) 222–223. Four handled Martial's works: In
addition to Tryphon, Atrectus, and Secundus, there was
Quintus Pollius Valerianus (Martial 1.113). Bookstores
stocked current authors as early as 20 B.C., as we can tell
from Horace's indication in *Epistulae* 1.20.2 that the work
was available for sale at the store run by the Sosii family; cf.

also *Epistulae* 2.3.345. "This little slender": 13.3.1–4. Atrectus: 1.117.10–17. Secundus: 1.2. "An author's copy": 4.72. Tryphon, publisher of Quintilian: Quintilian, *Praef.* Stores selling classics: See Seneca, *De Beneficiis* 7.6.1, where he mentions a bookdealer Dorus who had copies of Cicero and Livy for sale. Antiquarian bookstores: See R. Starr in *Phoenix* 44 (1990) 148–157. "exhibited for sale": 5.4.1.

106–108   Open sunrise to midday: An inscription found in the Athenian agora that probably came from the library of Pantainos there reads: "Open from the first hour to the sixth"; see R. Wycherley, *Agora iii* (Princeton 1957) 150, no. 464 and cf. Strocka 306. On these hours as the standard business hours, see E. Bickerman, *Chronology of the Ancient World* (Ithaca 1980²) 15. Capacity of bookcases: Cf. Packer i 454. Buckets: Called in Latin *scrinia* or *capsae*. Incident at Tibur: Gellius 19.5. Directors eliminate borrowing: In the inscription cited above, the hours of opening are preceded by the words "No book shall be taken out; we have [so] sworn." Aurelius' borrowing: P. Fedeli, in *Quaderni urbinati di cultura classica* 45 (1984) 165–168, cites Aurelius' letter as proof that Rome's libraries permitted borrowing; L. Piacente, in *Studi latini e italiani* 2 (1988) 56–57, argues that the borrowing in this case was a special privilege.

Chapter 7. Libraries of the Roman Empire: *Outside the City of Rome*

109–111   Pompeian graffiti: A. Mau, trans. F. Kelsey, *Pompeii: Its Life and Art* (New York 1899) 481–488. ABCs: *CIL* 4.2514–2548. Lines of Vergil: Mau and Kelsey 488. Citation of love poets: Mau and Kelsey 485; for citation of other poets, cf. L. Richardson in *Archaeology* 30 (1977) 395. Wall-paintings: Richardson 394. Library at Pompeii 400–402. Comum: *CIL* 5.5262. Suessa Aurunca: 10.4760. Volsinii: 11.2704.

111–113   Claudius' addition, his histories: Suetonius, *Claud.* 42.2. Untrustworthy informant: C. Calvisius Sabinus, cited by Plutarch, who notes that not all he said was believed (*Antony* 58–59). Library in Asclepius' sanctuary at Pergamum: Callmer 175–176; Strocka 320–322. Pantainos' library: 304–306. "Titus Flavius Pantainos . . . dedicated":

Platthy no. 36 (= R. Wycherley, *The Athenian Agora* iii [Princeton 1957] p. 150).

113–116 Hadrian's library: Callmer 172–174; Strocka 318–320. Library of Celsus: Callmer 170–171; Strocka 322–329; A. Boëthius and J. Ward-Perkins, *Etruscan and Roman Architecture* (Pelican History of Art 1970) 397, 398. "For Tiberius Julius Celsus": Platthy no. 128 (= *Forschungen in Ephesos* v [Vienna 1953] p. 75). 3,000 rolls: It has been estimated (Packer i 454) that the niches of Hadrian's library, 2.80 m high and 1.20 m wide, held ca. 120 rolls; those in Celsus' library, the same height but narrower (1 m), would have held ca. 100 rolls.

116–120 Only two libraries attested in west: Cf. Harris 273. Mention of library at Carthage: Apuleius, *Florida* 18.8. Carthage's renewal: *OCD*³ s.v. "Carthage." Library at Timgad: H. Pfeiffer in *Memoirs of the American Academy in Rome* 9 (1931) 157–165; Callmer 181–182. Pfeiffer (159) dates it 250 at the latest; in *OCD*³ s.v. "Thamugadi" it is dated fourth century. Spread of Latin language and Roman culture in the west: Cf. Harris 272. Schools in major towns: 242–244. Higher education: H. Marrou, trans. G. Lamb, *A History of Education in Antiquity* (London 1956) 297. Martial: He was born between 38 and 41 and did not leave for Rome until 64 (*OCD*³ 930). Lack of evidence for western libraries: Even for Spain, one of the most cultured areas of the Roman west, there is no evidence for the existence of public libraries; see the exhaustive study of C. Hanson, "Were There Libraries in Roman Spain?" *Libraries & Culture* 24 (1989) 198–216. Harris assumes (273) that only two were in existence and offers an unconvincing socio-political explanation of why so few.

121–122 Longianus: Platthy no. 132; *RE* s.v. "Iulius (no. 321)" (vol. x, p. 663). Doctor-poet: *Tituli Asiae Minoris* 2.3 (Vienna 1944) no. 910; *RE* Supplementband 4, p. 731. Quadrigarius: Gellius 9.14.3. Discovery at Patras: Gellius 18.9.5. Roman soldiers settled at Patras: Strabo 8.387.

Chapter 8. From Roll to Codex

124–125 "This bulky mass": Martial 14.192. *membranae* = "parchment codex": Cf. van Haelst 22. Editions of Vergil, Cicero,

Livy: 14.186, 188, 190. Writing tablets: Roberts-Skeat 11–14; van Haelst 14–17. Tablets of ten boards: Blanchard 57, 59. Roman invention of parchment notebook: Roberts-Skeat 15–23; van Haelst 18–20. Parchment notebook as step toward the codex: van Haelst 20. "How small a tablet": 14.186.

125–126 "Leather in many folds": 14.184. 550 codices, 60 percent papyrus, 40 percent parchment: See the statistics of finds published by W. Willis in *GRBS* 9 (1968) 220. Since the statistics here, as well as those in Roberts-Skeat, reflect finds only up to the date of publication and include items whose date is not strictly certain, to avoid a misleading impression of exactness, I use round numbers in the text and supply in the notes the numbers actually reported. Willis' actual figures total 536 codices, of which 389 are of papyrus and 147 of parchment. Subsequent finds undoubtedly will have raised these and the other numbers cited but almost certainly without affecting the ratios (cf. Roberts-Skeat 3).

127–128 1330 writings, 20 on codices: See the totals of finds by century in Roberts-Skeat 37; the figures for the first and second century total precisely 1,331 finds, of which 1,312 are rolls and 19 codices. Third century, A.D. 300, A.D. 400: Roberts-Skeat 37 gives for the period from the end of the second century to the early decades of the fourth 809 rolls and 160 codices; for around A.D. 300 54 rolls and 50 codices; for the fourth into the early decades of the fifth 43 rolls and 167 codices; for the rest of the fifth 11 rolls and 88 codices. Continued life of rolls: Lewis 90–94.

128 Make-up of codices: Turner 13–14. Extreme example: Papyrus Bodmer II, a copy of the Gospel of John dating ca. 200; cf. Turner ibid.

129 Greater capacity of the codex: Cf. Roberts-Skeat 48. Convenient for travelers: See Martial 1.2 cited **104** above (codex edition of his own works), 14.188 (of Cicero). Ease of access to contents: Cf. Turner 8; Roberts-Skeat 50 (whose remarks on the ancients' carelessness about exact citation do not alter the fact that the codex allowed easier access). Covers: Turner 14. Titles: Cf. Wilson 54–55 (examples of codices with titles painted on fore-edge); Turner 7 (labels on rolls liable to fall off). Reluctance of readers and scriptoria to change to codex: Cf. Roberts-Skeat 73–74.

129–130   Christian preference for the codex: Roberts-Skeat 38–44, 62–66; van Haelst 23–28. Favored the codex for non-Biblical religious writings: Roberts-Skeat 42–44. Eleven early Bibles: Roberts-Skeat 40–41; van Haelst 28. 1,200 pagan writings, 30 codices: See the statistics in Roberts-Skeat 37, where the exact figures add up to 1,206 and 31. Rises to 170: See Roberts-Skeat 38, where the exact figure is 172. Sole exceptional instance: Roberts-Skeat 39–40.

130   Codex adopted by Christians at Rome: Cf. van Haelst 34–35; see also Roberts-Skeat 58–60 (arguments in favor of Antioch) and van Haelst 31–32 (objections). Free of associations of roll: Cf. Roberts-Skeat 56, 60.

131   Eighteen codices, four of parchment: See van Haelst 23–25. "Deios came to us": U. Hagedorn et al., *Das Archiv des Petaus* (Köln 1969) no. 30; van Haelst 21–23. Third century finds: See the statistics in Willis (op. cit. under **125–126** above) 220, where the precise total is 105, of which fifteen are Greek parchment codices and two Latin. Fourth, fifth centuries: See Willis ibid., where the precise figures are: for the fourth century, 160 total of which 56 are parchment; for the fifth century, 152 total of which 46 are parchment.

131–132   Jerome, *Epistulae* 34 (J.-P. Migne, *Patrologia Latina*, vol. 22, 448). Constantine's letter: Eusebius, *Vita Constantini* 4.36 (Migne, *Patrologia Graeca*, vol. 20, 1185). Largest surviving papyrus Bible codex: The Chester Beatty papyrus of the Gospels and Acts; see Turner 15. Letter of St. Basil: *Ep.* 231 (Migne, *Patrologia Graeca*, vol. 32, 861; R. Deferrari, *The Fathers of the Church*, vol 28, 158). Latin poet: *Epigrammata Bobiensia* no. 57.

132–133   Bible copies: Codex Sinaiticus, Codex Vaticanus. Latin authors: E. Lowe, *Codices Latini Antiquiores*, Part 1 (Oxford 1934) nos. 11, 13, 19 (Vergil); 12 (Terence); 27 (Fronto). Homer: Codex Ambrosianus; cf. E. Thompson, *An Introduction to Greek and Latin Palaeography* (Oxford 1912) 198–199. Papyrus no longer qualified for luxury books: Cf. Turner 16. Parchment codices as law school textbooks: A. Norman in *JHS* 80 (1960) 124. Make a student's knees sag: Libanius, *Orationes* 4.18. Missile in student fights: *Orationes* 58.5.

133 Pliny's letter: *Epistulae* 3.5. Ride in a litter rather than walk: 3.5.15–16. Have books read: 3.5.10.

Chapter 9. Toward the Middle Ages

136–137 Destructive warfare, Rome's minimal population: R. Krautheimer, *Rome, Profile of a City, 312–1308* (Princeton 1980) 62–65. Eastern empire fared better: A. Jones, *The Later Roman Empire 284–602* (Oxford 1964) 1027–1031. Professorial chairs: *Codex Theodosianus* 14.9.3; cf. Jones 990–991.

137–139 Constantinople's libraries: Wilson 54–58. Serapaeum library: See the convenient presentation by J. Thiem in *Journal of the History of Ideas* 40 (1979) 508–511. Collection at Jerusalem: Leclercq 857. Eusebius' comments: *Historia Ecclesiastica* 6.20. Collection at Caesarea: Leclercq 857; T. Tanner in *Journal of Library History* 14 (1979) 418–419.

139–141 Libraries at Rome: Leclercq 866–872; Thompson 21–22, 140. Mural of St. Augustine: Leclercq 869–870, with illustration in color opp. 868. Seventh-century date: Cf. Krautheimer (op. cit. under **136–137** above) 54. Attitude toward pagan literature: Jones (op. cit. under **136–137** above) 1005–1006; P. Lejay, "Latin Literature in the Church," *The Catholic Encyclopedia* (New York 1910) ix 32. Jerome's dream: *Epist.* 22.30 (J.-P. Migne, *Patrologia Latina*, vol. 22, 416). Gregory the Great's attitude: Jones 1005. Collections in Spain with pagan works: Leclercq 876 (library of St. Braulio). Isidore: Thompson 28; J. Clark, *The Care of Books* (Cambridge 1902) 47–48. Ban on monks' reading: *Regula Monachorum* 8 (Migne, *Pat. Lat.*, vol. 83, 877–878). Verses: Clark, ibid.; Migne, *Pat. Lat.*, vol. 83, 1107–1111.

141–142 Pachomius: W. Smith, *Dictionary of Greek and Roman Biography and Mythology* (London 1856) s.v. "Pachomius." "is ignorant of letters": *Regula Pachomii* 139–140 (J.-P. Migne, *Patrologia Latina*, vol. 23, 82). Rule concerning books: *Reg. Pach.* 100 (Migne vol. 23, 78); cf. Clark (op. cit. under **139–141** above) 54–55. Scant information on eastern libraries: Wilson 53. Monastery collections at Constantinople: Wilson 63–64. Patmos: Wilson 69–70; S. Padover in Thompson 323–324. Byzantine private libraries: E.g., of Photion and Arethas; see Padover 317–319.

142–144   Benedict's stipulations concerning reading: *Regula* 48. "since all in the city": Sulpicius Severus, *Dial.* 1.23. Books for Britain from Rome: Thompson 25–26. Cassiodorus' purchases from north Africa: *Inst.* 1.8 (J.-P. Migne, *Patrologia Latina*, vol. 70, 1120); cf. *An Introduction to Divine and Human Readings by Cassiodorus Senator*, trans. with introd. by L. Jones (New York 1946) 33. Cassiodorus' public life: Jones 7–19. Younger monks do copying: Sulpicius Severus, *Life of St. Martin* 7 (referring to St. Martin's monastery at Tours). Copying done by the unfit: Ferreolus, *Regula ad Monachos* 28 (Migne, *Pat. Lat.*, vol. 66, 969). "with his hand preaches": *Inst.* 1.30 (Migne, *Pat. Lat.*, 70, 1144–1145). Copying of secular literature: Jones 35. *De Orthographia*: Jones 41. Vivarium's library: Leclercq 877–878; Thompson 40.

145   *Institutiones* widely owned: L. Jones (op. cit. under **142– 144** above) 48, 50–53. Bobbio: Thompson 44–48. St. Gallen: 83–84. Fulda: 67–72. Petrarch: 524–527. Medici: 544–549.

Illustrations

Index